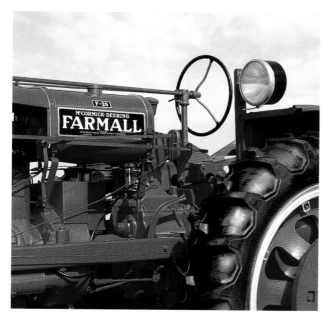

Vintage
International
Harvester
Tractors

Ralph W. Sanders

TOWN
SQUARE
BOOKS

an imprint of Voyageur Press

Dedication

To Joanne, my bride of nearly forty years, for her constant love, support, and companionship

---

Edited by Michael Dregni
Designed by Andrea Rud
Printed in Hong Kong

97 98 99 00 01 5 4 3 2 1

Library of Congress Cataloging-in-Publication Data
Sanders, Ralph W., 1933–
     Vintage International Harvester tractors / by Ralph W.
     Sanders.
        p.   cm.
     Includes bibliographical references (p. 157) and index.
     ISBN 0-89658-355-4
     1. IHC tractors—History. 2. Farm tractors—United
States—History. 3. International Harvester Company. I. Title.
TL233.6.I38S26 1997
629.225'2—dc21   97-6793
                                CIP

A Town Square Book
Published by Voyageur Press, Inc.
123 North Second Street, P.O. Box 338
Stillwater, MN 55082 U.S.A.
612-430-2210, fax 612-430-2211

Distributed in Europe by
Midland Publishing Ltd.
24 The Hollow, Earl Shilton
Leicester LE9 7NA, England
Tel: 01455 233747

Educators, fundraisers, premium and gift buyers, publicists, and marketing managers: Looking for creative products and new sales ideas? Voyageur Press books are available at special discounts when purchased in quantities, and special editions can be created to your specifications. For details contact the marketing department at 800-888-9653.

Permissions
Most of the black and white photographs illustrating this book are from the McCormick–International Harvester Company Collection and are used with permission of the State Historical Society of Wisconsin, Madison, Wisconsin, where the IH collection is housed.

Some of the line cuts of historic farm equipment are reprinted from Paul C. Johnson's 1978 book *Farm Power in the Making of America* with the kind permission of the Institute for Agricultural Biodiversity (IAB) of Decorah, Iowa.

Some of the color photographs in this book were first printed in the DuPont *Classic Farm Tractors* calendars of 1990 through 1993, and are used here with the kind permission of E. I. Du Pont de Nemours and Company, Wilmington, Delaware.

VHS videotapes featuring the tractors and owners from *Classic Farm Tractors* calendars of 1990 through 1996 can be ordered from Venard Films, Ltd., Box 1332, Peoria, Illinois 61654. Telephone (309) 699-3911.

Classic Farm Tractors calendars are published by Calendar Promotions, Inc., 1010 South Ninth St., Washington, Iowa 52353. Telephone (319) 653-6535.

Page 2: *IH 8/16 tractor and Model F truck*
Page 3, inset: *Farmall 30*

Contents

Farmall F-30 literature

Acknowledgments

International Harvester tractors from many areas of North America are pictured in the photographs in this book. I initially created many of the formal color photographs of farm tractors for use in *Classic Farm Tractors* calendars produced annually by Calendar Promotions, Inc., of Washington, Iowa. My thanks to Jim Ratcliff of Calendar Promotions and John Harvey of John Harvey Communications, Wilmington, Delaware, calendar originator and co-ordinator, for their help in making this book possible.

Most of the black-and-white tractor photographs are from the McCormick–International Harvester Company Collection at the State Historical Society of Wisconsin, and are used here with permission. Special thanks to the Historical Society and IH archives staff for their help in locating important documents, papers, and photos, especially to Cynthia Knight, Archivist; Nicolette Bromberg, Visual Curator; Scott Portman; Andy Kraushaar; David Benjamin; and other archives staff members for all of their help.

Other book illustrations are from farm magazines of the period as well as IH brochures and advertising material collected from a variety of sources.

For all of their cooperation, time, and patience, I want to thank the tractor owners whose IH machines I photographed during the past ten years. These people include: Max Armstrong, Naperville, Illinois; John Bossler, Highland, Illinois; James and Gladys Gall, Reserve, Kansas; Alton and Thalua Garner, Levelland, Texas; Harold Glaus, Nashville, Tennessee; Verlan Heberer, Belleville, Illinois; Roland Henik, Mt. Vernon, Iowa; Tom Hill, Piqua, Ohio; Jon Kinzenbaw, Williamsburg, Iowa; Robert Lessen, Hartsburg, Illinois; Rex Miller, Savannah, Missouri; Purdue University Agricultural Engineering Department, West Lafayette, Indiana; Don Rimathe, Huxley, Iowa; Roger and Howard Schnell, Franklin Grove, Illinois; Clem Seivert, Granger, Iowa; Lawrance N. Shaw, Gainesville, Florida; Merrill Sheets, Delaware, Ohio; Alan Smith, McHenry, Illinois; Powell Smith, Shelbyville, Tennessee; Phil, Bill, and Glen Stewart, Springport, Michigan; Wes Stratman, Pueblo, Colorado; and the University of Nebraska Tractor Test Station Museum, Lincoln, Nebraska.

Not only did the tractor owners give unstintingly of their time, but their knowledge of their favorite machines provided a great background in assembling the information for the book's text. Some of them offered printed literature that explains their tractor's role in the International Harvester story. That material has helped the story and is greatly appreciated.

In addition to the tractor owners there were also many other people collaborating behind the scenes to help make the photos successful. For the downtown Chicago shot of Max Armstrong's Super H Farmall, thanks go first to Max Armstrong for his idea of showing off his tractor in a metropolitan setting just off Michigan Avenue in Chicago near the spot where Cyrus H. McCormick's first reaper works was located. Next, thanks to his tractor's restorer, Don Corrie of Chenoa, Illinois, for his sparkling restoration of the Super H Farmall. Wayne and Loretta Withers of Newark, Illinois, transported the tractor to the chosen spot in the pre-dawn blackness that Sunday morning in June. At the photo site, two of Chicago's finest police officers worked with us, suggested a good location for the photography, and kept us out of trouble during the shoot. My wife, Joanne, and our Chicago-dwelling son, Neil Sanders, helped with onsite logistics including a quick tire dusting and pick up and disposal of overnight debris. So with a lot of help and a lot of luck, our efforts succeeded. That day dawned fair and warm. Perfect for photography. We all know who gets credit for that. By nine that morning, we were done and gone. Thanks be to all!

Not always do photo shoots go that smoothly. That's where persistence comes in. There are rainy days and rainy weeks, rainy months, and even rainy years. Verlan Heberer of Belleville, Illinois, and I scheduled his orchard tractor for photography several times over a two-year period before we finally picked the right day. We found that sometimes apple trees don't bloom on schedule or the blooms disappear in wind or rain. We finally picked a gorgeous fall day with apples on the trees to show his McCormick O-4 in its working environment. Heberer was generous with his time and so was his paint specialist, Rick Scheibel of Mascoutah, Illinois, in getting the pictures on the chosen day. Thanks are also due orchard owner Floyd Schlueter for letting us use his trees as background. Several other illustrations in the book are from a 1923 McCormick-Deering dealer catalog generously loaned by Heberer.

John Bossler of Highland, Illinois, loaned brochures and sales literature from which some of the illustrations for the Farmall F series tractors were taken. Thank you, John.

Some of the line cuts of early McCormick and International equipment, are from Paul C. Johnson's book *Farm Power in the Making of America* last published by the Institute for Agricultural Biodiversity (IAB) at Decorah, Iowa. IAB runs a conservation program for endangered farm animal breeds and shows some of them at its Farm Park at 730 College Drive, Decorah, IA 52101. The late Paul C. Johnson was a long-time editor of *Prairie Farmer* magazine, the venerable farm magazine with continuous roots going back to 1841. It was my good fortune to have had Paul as a boss and mentor during my stint at *Prairie Farmer* from 1964 until 1968.

Since my farm debut in 1933 provided no experience with horse farming, I have leaned heavily on the experiences of my father-in-law, Lester W. Helms of rural Belleville, Illinois. His entry into the world in 1906 (the year the first IH tractor barked to life) put him on the seat behind his father's teams by about 1915 and provided him with tales of farming with horsepower pre-tractor. Thanks for sharing, Dad!

My thanks go too to Michael Dregni, Editorial Director at Voyageur Press, whose guidance and editing skills helped keep me on track and made this book readable and meaningful. Thanks again, Michael!

Ralph W. Sanders
West Des Moines, Iowa

The Power of the Hour

Power is the big factor that insures success on the farm to-day. With plenty of power the seed beds can be thoroughly prepared and the crops put in on time. Both of these help to insure bigger and better yields and surer profits.

A Titan 10-20 kerosene tractor will supply that needed power at the lowest possible figure. It will step in and take the heavy burdens off your horses.

Titan 10-20 is made for the hardest kinds of farm work. Farmers everywhere have learned the advantages of its low-speed, long-life, completely enclosed motor; mechanical lubricator that always supplies the needed amount of oil; the famous Titan kerosene mixer that uses kerosene or distillate down to 39 degrees Baum; the magneto that is so perfected that the tractor starts and runs without the use of batteries; and many other important features that are completely described in our catalogue, which we will gladly send you.

International Harvester Company of Australia Pty. Ltd.

229-231 Castlereagh St., SYDNEY

Australian ad for the Titan 10/20

Introduction

Goodbye Horses, Hello Farmall

I was a small boy of five on the home farm in Illinois when the day came. At breakfast one morning in early spring 1938, my father suggested I help him spread manure that day. I was young enough that it was an honor to "help" Dad with anything—and at that age I had little experience with the tough job that manure loading could be. I remember now, from later experience, it was a job you attached yourself to by grabbing an ash handle whose business end was four steel prongs, and then digging in. Right hand low on the handle for lifting and the left hand high on the handle for control in the throw.

Author at three.

My older brother Jack was in school and my younger brother Jim was not yet three. Jim, although also willing to help Dad, was "needed" to "help" Mother in the house. So I was honored and anxious to be Dad's helper that chilly morning. It's taken me sixty years and some thoughtful reflection to figure out why he needed my help in the barn that day. After all, a five-year-old can't fork much hay-tangled, cattle-packed manure.

While Dad went to the barn and harnessed the team to the old Emerson-Brantingham manure spreader, Mother helped me find and don my coat, hat, and mittens, and I was off to the barn. There in the west driveway, where the feeder cattle fed on the alfalfa hay pitched into the bunks from the hay mow above, was Dad, the team, and the spreader. Dad was already hard at work filling the spreader with great overhanging forkfuls of steaming manure. I helped as I could, mainly by staying out of his way. I may have even held the horses. They were a gentle pair.

About the time Dad had the spreader mounded full, a stranger (to me) came to the barn. He wanted to see the horses work, Dad explained to me later. So sitting side-by-side on the spreader seat, Dad and I drove to the field south of the barn, put the spreader in gear with the lever beside the seat, adjusted the speed of the unloading apron with the other lever, and began to spread out the load.

All this time the stranger walked alongside and carefully watched the horses as they plodded along, leaning well into the harness as they pulled the heavy spreader and its spinning beater. It was a quiet scene with only the rhythmic metallic clanks of the ratchet that moved the apron and the whir of the spreader beaters as they tore through the manure and flung it randomly to the rear. The team knew their job. They pulled the load steadily without protest and with only clucks of encouragement from Dad.

I must have gotten cold and headed to the house once we got back to the barn, since I have no recollection of the conversation that must have ensued between Dad and the stranger. I certainly would have perked up my ears and paid attention had I known what they were talking about.

I had forgotten the events of that morning until one afternoon days later when I heard a laboring truck shifting through its gears coming up our long gravel driveway. I was supposed to be taking a nap (mandatory until the age of six at the Sanders farm) but I had to investigate. When I looked out of the second floor window of "the boy's room" to the driveway below, I saw a stock-rack-equipped truck hauling a gray tractor with red steel wheels. Squeezed in beside the front of the tractor was a cultivator and some other implement. Could that tractor be ours or was the driver just lost and looking for another farm?

Obedient son that I was, I stayed in the bedroom pretending to nap. Sometime later, the truck started again, and when I peeked down as it passed the house on its way out the lane, the story began to fall into place. Even a five-year-old could figure out most of it. Our last team had been loaded into the truck and our horses were leaving the farm. The tractor had been unloaded—it was staying!

Our "new" tractor was a five-year-old F-12 Farmall on steel wheels with a two-row front-mounted cultivator and a rear-mounted sickle-bar mower. Dad had traded the last team—the one he had kept for cultivating corn—on the F-12. The stranger (probably the tractor dealer or his salesman) that had watched the horses spread manure just wanted to see them work to ensure their soundness before making the deal on the tractor. Dad was probably just as cautious about negotiating a deal with return privileges on the tractor in case it didn't work out.

Dad took some good-natured ribbing about the swap from my Uncle Bain, mother's brother. "John," he said, "you shouldn't have traded your last horses for a tractor. Now you're going to raise three sons that won't know how to harness a team." Convinced he had done the right thing, Dad answered laconically, "Yes, Bain, but I never learned to yoke oxen, and I seem to be getting by."

By the time I was ten, the same age as the F-12, it had been equipped with Montgomery Ward Riverside knob-tread rubber tires and a high gear that gave it a blistering top speed of 5 mph (8 km/h)—if you pulled hard enough on the notched throttle rod. The F-12 tractor became "my" tractor when my legs were long enough that I could push in the clutch without sliding all the way off the seat.

With it I could do a lot of the light tractor work, including spike-tooth harrowing-down of rough spring-plowed ground. With a four-section harrow, that was sometimes a heavy pull. Plowing with the F-12 and a two fourteen-inch (35-cm) plow was an experience. The plow was too big for the tractor—two twelve-inch (30-cm) bottoms would have been better, and two ten-inch ideal.

Dad used sweet clover as the legume interplanted in the small grain in the crop rotation. The sweet clover was often pastured when it was held over for a year in the corn, soybeans, wheat, or oats on a four-year crop rotation. Plowing under the rank sweet clover with the F-12 provided the spectacle of getting stuck on every cow pie the knobby-tired left wheel encountered. Only by using the hand brakes on that side to transfer power to the right wheel could I get the rig moving again. Stubble and pasture clipping with the mounted mower was fun. The F-12 let you cut square corners without slowing down.

As we grew up with the tractor one of our tests of our young manhood was to have the strength to "spin" (or continuously turn) the starting crank. We three Sanders boys could soon spin the crank at will. We were either getting stronger or the tractor was getting weaker and needed a ring job.

Dad always drove the tractor to plant and cultivate corn, both critical operations. My brothers and I lacked the needed skills to plant checkrowed corn and were short of the back strength needed to manually lift the F-12's lever-operated cultivator.

We used the hardy little F-12 tractor through World War II. It got some relief about 1944 when Dad added a Ford-Ferguson 2N to our three-tractor fleet. Heavy tillage was done with a four-plow gasoline Caterpillar R-2.

The gray F-12 (looking black by then) was traded for a shiny new red Farmall C about 1948. With its hydraulic implement lift, starter, lights, ease of driving, good seat, and superior visibility, the C was a pleasure to operate. During my last three years in high school and my first two years of college, I cultivated a lot of corn on the farm each summer with the Farmall C. Unlike the horses, the C was never traded; it's still on the farm where it helps do chores for my older brother Jack.

And what has been finally revealed to me after sixty years? Not only was my father anxious to share his time with me as a boy of five that early spring morning, but he also wanted me to witness a great change that was occurring on the farm in our lifetimes, that of the passing of horses from use on farms. I didn't figure it out in time to thank him for that. But I will always be grateful I was there with him that day to share the experience.

Facing page, top: **1932 Farmall F-12 pre-production**
Facing page, bottom: **1939 Farmall F-14**

Chapter 1

The
Virginia
Reaper

The social importance of the reaper was
that it substituted horse-power for the tired
muscles of straining peasants. . . .
—Cyrus McCormick III,
The Century of the Reaper, 1931

Historic Chicago site
Left: *A 1953 Farmall Super H poses proudly in downtown*
Chicago, Illinois, in front of the site where famed Virginia
inventor Cyrus McCormick built his first reaper factory. The
reaper revolutionized grain harvest around the globe.
McCormick's Reaper Works of 1848 was located on the north
bank of the Chicago River just east of Michigan Avenue. The
Equitable Building, centered behind the Farmall, occupies two
of the three lots on which McCormick's Reaper Works was
located. IH was headquartered in the Equitable Building for
many years.

The International Harvester Company, originator of the famous Farmall tractor, boasts a rich history. The story traces back some 170 years to a labor-saving device that changed the agricultural development of the western world. The simple machine was the grain reaper, created by Scotch-Irish inventor-farmer Cyrus Hall McCormick and hammered out on a stone anvil in 1831 within sight of the misty Blue Ridge Mountains of Virginia. McCormick later built a worldwide business based on his famous reaper, a business that in 1902 became the backbone of the huge IH.

Cyrus McCormick was born February 15, 1809, the first son of Robert McCormick and Mary Ann Hall McCormick. They had seven other children, including Cyrus's brothers, William S. and Leander J., who would also play major roles in developing and marketing the McCormick reaper.

Cyrus's father, Robert, was an inventive entrepreneur. His farm was home to an assortment of enterprises including a blacksmith shop, grist mill, sawmill, lime kiln, and even a distillery, where Robert sold whiskey for 25 cents per gallon.

The elder McCormick devised and patented a hemp break, and young Cyrus worked with his father to develop markets for the tool. Hemp was grown for its use in cordage and rough fabrics. Robert's new hemp break broke the hemp fibers out of the plant stalks, a key step in processing the plant for use.

Robert had also invented several other machines and tried his hand at making a reaper off and on from 1816 through 1831. He apparently gave up that project and let Cyrus try his own ideas.

Cyrus was but twenty-two years old when he first tried out his frail-looking reaper in July 1831 on a six-acre (2.4-hectare) field of oats at Steele's Tavern, near his family home of Walnut Grove in the Shenandoah Valley of Virginia. The rudimentary reaper worked well enough in John Steele's oats to encourage the young man to continue development.

In 1834, young Cyrus received patent protection on his machine's features, but only after a similar machine was patented earlier by Obed Hussey on December 31, 1833. Hussey's machine is credited with originating the sectioned sickles still used on combines and mowers. McCormick's lasting contributions include the revolving reel and divider board.

Whether Cyrus is the "inventor" of the reaper is a moot point. Like Illinois steel-plow maker John Deere,

Cyrus got his individual product accepted, got it manufactured, and got it sold to and used by an expanding number of satisfied farmers.

The Pig Iron Venture

Robert and Cyrus McCormick were nearly lead astray from the path of developing the reaper. The lure of a new business off the farm tempted father and son into an iron furnace venture in 1836 that nearly cost them the home farm. Cotopaxi, as their furnace was called, certainly distracted them from the immediate development of the reaper. They started off with high hopes for big profits, but pig-iron prices soon plunged from a high of $50 to $55 per ton in Richmond, Virginia, as they began building their iron furnace, to $40 per ton, and then skidded to $25 per ton when they began to pour iron in the summer of 1837, just as that year's financial panic took hold. Finding enough wood to convert into charcoal for the furnace and other production problems plagued the struggling enterprise already stymied by the low prices.

After five years, Cyrus and Robert gave up on the iron furnace business and got out by leasing the furnace to others. It was a powerful learning experience for Cyrus. Tradition says he emerged from it with his honor, one slave, a horse and saddle, and $300. But it took years to pay back money borrowed on Walnut Grove to support the furnace. That money apparently came from the sale of previously unsold iron and from the reapers that then sold for about $100 each.

From that debacle forward, Cyrus was never diverted from his cause and pursued only the reaper business. The Cotopaxi fiasco had given him a crash course in iron, marketing, management of workmen, and business ethics, as well as law and court procedure. He used the "schooling" to good advantage, and the reaper business began to grow, especially when his machine was well received in the newly developing wheat-growing areas of the American Midwest.

The Reaper Heads West

Cyrus continued to improve and demonstrate his original Virginia Reaper, and its reputation spread outside his own Rockbridge County. The McCormicks began to fill orders for reapers from their farm shops in about 1840. Cyrus was to get patent royalties of $15 per machine from the reapers made at Walnut Grove. From all accounts, Cyrus was in charge

Cradlers in wheat

Small grain harvest was labor intensive before the invention of the reaper. Each good worker with a cradle could cut up to three acres (1.2 hectares) per day. The cut grain was next gathered into bundles, bound, then shocked. Laboring in the heat of mid-summer, workers in the Shenandoah Valley of Virginia drank water flavored with molasses and ginger to help maintain their energy. "Ra-al Monongehely" was made with one gallon of sorghum molasses dissolved in five gallons of water spiced with a quarter pound of ginger. (Photo courtesy State Historical Society of Wisconsin #WHiI-71-S)

of sales and demonstrations and traveled to develop markets for the labor-saving device. The Virginia Reaper was said to save half the labor needed for hand harvesting.

McCormick sparred and feuded over ideas and sales territory with Obed Hussey and his reaper until Hussey died in a train accident in 1860. Hussey's machine was described as superior at mowing, and was well regarded in the eastern farming areas. A later reaper competitor, John H. Manny, was a target of McCormick's competitive spirit years later in Illinois. Manny's machine laid the foundation for the Emerson-Brantingham Company of Rockford, Illinois. E-B was acquired in 1928 by J. I. Case Company, Inc.

McCormick worked for sixteen years on his 1831 invention. The Virginian developed his new machine,

sought suitable manufacturers, fended off imitators, and honed his skills as a marketer. By 1848, McCormick had made and sold about 1,278 reapers, most of which were built by other makers licensed by McCormick. Workers at the blacksmith shop at the McCormick's Walnut Grove home, where the first reaper was crafted, continued to make a few reapers each year for the local Virginia trade until manufacture ended there in 1847, the year after the death of McCormick's father, Robert.

In late 1847, McCormick signed a partnership agreement with harvesting cradle maker Charles M. Gray of Chicago. The new firm, McCormick & Gray, bought three lots on the north bank of the Chicago River near the pier "a few rods west of the Lake House," on which to build its reaper factory. The firm bought the 100-yard (90-meter) river frontage for

$25,000 from William B. Ogden, an early mayor of the city and prominent financier who was later a short-term McCormick partner. Today, the site of McCormick's original factory lies just east of the Michigan Avenue bridge, where the high-rise Equitable Building now stands, at 401 North Michigan Avenue.

The city of Chicago grew from less than 17,000 residents in 1847, to soon become the bustling giant of the prairie. McCormick's company grew up with the city to become the foundation of the gigantic farm implement maker, International Harvester. Cincinnati, Ohio, might have been chosen but for the warm reception the reaper earned in the "West."

Cyrus was thirty-nine years old when the new Chicago factory began making machines beside the Chicago River in 1848, just some 150 years ago. First patented in 1834, his reaper's original patents were to expire in 1848, the year reaper production began in Chicago. Despite his unceasing efforts over the next ten years, Cyrus's appeals to get his original patents extended were denied and other reaper makers freely used his original principles. Competition was heating up, but McCormick was up to the challenge.

McCormick bought out his first Chicago partner, Gray, in fall 1848. In 1849, McCormick signed a partnership with William B. Ogden and a Mr. Jones to create McCormick, Ogden & Co., which lasted a year. Orloff M. Dorman became McCormick's partner in 1850, but he too was bought out by McCormick at year's end. McCormick operated his business without partners beginning in 1851, the year after his brothers William and Leander joined him in Chicago as employees.

The reaper shop had a good first year. By fall 1848, all but thirteen of the 500 reapers made in the new Chicago facility were sold, and Cyrus netted some $30,000 in profits. Cyrus was finally onto a good thing and business was rolling. The year 1849 was better yet as production and sales nearly tripled. In 1850, reaper sales amounted to almost 1,600 units. In 1851, the shop became a true factory when a 30-hp steam engine was installed to operate the lineshaft-driven power equipment used to make reapers.

From 1831 to 1851, about 5,200 McCormick reapers were built. The Chicago factory continued to grow and add capacity despite an economic slump from 1851 through 1853 when only about 1,000 reapers

Cyrus Hall McCormick
Reaper inventor Cyrus Hall McCormick didn't live to see the formation of International Harvester. He died in Chicago on May 13, 1884. That year his company sold more than 58,000 machines and introduced its steel twine binder.

were sold annually. By the end of 1856, Cyrus's profits for the year rose to nearly $300,000. By 1858, ten years after he had started making his own reapers, McCormick could claim the then lofty status of being a millionaire.

Brothers Share the Profits

In late 1859, a partnership with brothers William and Leander was formed as C. H. McCormick & Bros. William and Leander were to get salaries of $5,000 each and a quarter of the firm's profits. The product line was expanded in 1860 with the addition of a mower crafted by William. By the start of the American Civil War in 1861, the Chicago McCormick Reaper Works employed some 1,000 workers making about 5,000 machines annually. A second partnership agreement between the three brothers was signed in 1864, rais-

Atkins Automaton reaper
Competing machines challenged McCormick from time to time, and in 1852, the Virginian threatened to enter the farm publication business himself when Prairie Farmer *publisher and editor John S. Wright of Chicago began making the Atkins Automaton reaper in direct competition with McCormick. Wright was enjoying brisk sales in 1856 selling some 3,000 machines a year until disaster struck in 1857. Many of his Automaton reapers that year were mistakenly made from green wood that warped and ruined the machines. Wright was ruined too in trying to make the machines right. He lost his magazine and the reaper business due to green lumber. Wright's editorial and advertising support of McCormick had first helped him become established in Chicago.*

The Virginia reaper
McCormick first demonstrated his reaper to friends and relatives in John Steele's oat field near Steele's Tavern, Virginia, in July 1831. This artist's version of the historic event shows a single horse pulling the simple reaper as a raker walks beside the machine pulling cut grain off the platform onto the ground for later bundling and shocking. McCormick's machine employed a revolving reel that both pushed the grain into a reciprocating saw-toothed blade for cutting and then transferred the cut grain onto the platform where it accumulated until it was raked onto the ground. His early reaper could cut up to ten acres (4 hectares) per day and save half the labor used in cradle harvesting. McCormick delayed patenting his machine until June 21, 1834, less than a year after rival Obed Hussey patented his machine late, in 1833. (Photo courtesy State Historical Society of Wisconsin #Whi (X3) 50588)

ing salaries for William and Leander to $6,000 per year and requiring the two brothers to share in capital contributions to each receive a one-quarter portion of profits. Cyrus, as the major investor, got half the profit.

William McCormick died in November 1865. When his estate was settled, his heirs were paid $400,000 in 1869 for William's part of the business. Working under a stormy relationship, Leander and Cyrus remained in partnership when real trouble befell them.

The Great Chicago Fire
Whether or not it was Mrs. Patrick O'Leary's cow that kicked over the lantern and started the infamous Chicago fire of October 8–9, 1871, nearly 2,100 acres (840 hectares) of the Windy City burned. Almost 300 people died in the fire and 90,000 were left homeless. Property loss was estimated at $200 million—close to a third of the city's wealth. McCormick's plant too was consumed, and the fire loss included nearly 2,000 completed reapers and mowers.

After insurance settlements, the company's loss still amounted to $600,000. The good news was that the company vault protected the firm's records, fortunately including the valuable accounts receivable files so that the long list of customer accounts could be collected. McCormick's practice from the start was

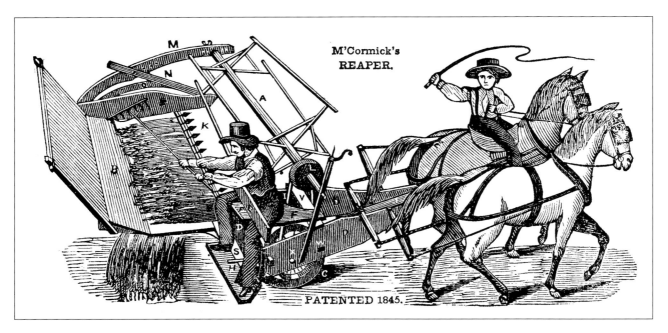

1845 McCormick reaper
A seat for the raker and other improvements were added to the machine McCormick patented in 1845. New too were an improved sickle and sickle guides, a hitch for a team of horses, and improvements to the reel. The raker's seat was modified in 1847 and patented before the machine was built in Chicago starting in 1848.

to generously extend credit to reaper customers, and accounts were now vigorously collected. Also on the plus side of the ledger were some 4,000 reapers already shipped and in agents' hands.

Cyrus McCormick was a sixty-two-year-old multimillionaire yet his factory lay in ashes. To rebuild or not? With a personal fortune nearing $6.5 million, money was not a problem. With a nod from Cyrus's wife, Nettie Fowler McCormick, a savvy business person, they returned to Chicago from New York, where they had been living to be near the nation's financial center, and went back to work. Fortunately, the company had recently bought more than 152 acres (60 hectares) a few miles southwest of downtown as a possible expansion site. Another 120 acres (48 hectares) were added and plans were soon made to build a much larger plant on the new site. The new McCormick Reaper Works was built on the south branch of the Chicago River in Canalport on Blue Island Avenue near Western Avenue.

Up From the Ashes

By January 1873, the new, modern factory was ready to resume production of the McCormick line of reapers, mowers, and harvesters. Powered by a 300-hp steam engine, implement construction would now be more efficient and at a much higher rate of production. The factory's location in the muddy fields a few miles southwest of downtown Chicago caused its share of problems until plank roads and other paving allowed nearly normal transportation. Once in full production, the new factory could produce about twice as many machines—up to 15,000 annually—as could the old plant that burned in the great fire.

Cyrus and his wife now had time to build their long-delayed Chicago home. It was built on a large lot they had held for many years at 675 Rush Street, and was finished in 1879 at a cost of about $175,000. Once completed, the three-story turreted brownstone was the talk of the city with its steam heat, gas lights, and ceiling frescoes.

Company sales rose to 22,000 units in 1880 and profits soared to $1 million. By the time of his death on May 13, 1884, at age 75, Cyrus McCormick's plant produced more than 50,000 machines annually.

Cyrus was succeeded as president of McCormick Harvesting Machine Company in 1890 by his son, Cyrus Hall McCormick II, after an acrimonious

Chicago factory

McCormick built his reaper factory on the north bank of the Chicago River, just east of the Michigan Avenue bridge, starting in fall 1847. Reaper production began in 1848 with 500 machines made and continued until the site was laid waste by the great Chicago fire of October 1871. Although about 2,000 reapers and mowers were destroyed by the fire, McCormick had already shipped some 4,000 reapers to his agents in other cities, so he had inventory with which to rebuild his business. (Photo courtesy State Historical Society of Wisconsin #WHiI-1511-T)

power struggle with Leander and his son, Robert Hall McCormick. Leander's and Robert's interests were bought out by Cyrus II and his mother for an estimated $3.25 million in 1890.

The curtains then opened on a new era of McCormick leadership in farm mechanization and its resulting increase in farm productivity and farm labor efficiency. As the nineteenth century came to an end, more sweeping changes were signaled by the intense war for harvester sales.

The Harvester Wars

As the twentieth century dawned, McCormick Harvesting Machine was the largest of its kind, but competitors had begun to close in. Chief among the competitors was Deering Harvester Company, located in Chicago unnervingly close to the McCormick operations. William Deering, a wealthy Yankee dry goods businessman from Maine, had also pegged his business on reapers, mowers, and harvesters, and was in direct competition with McCormick's machines.

In 1870, William Deering had invested $40,000 in a company owned by William Gannon that made the highly regarded Marsh harvester. The Marsh was invented by the Marsh brothers of Shabbona Grove, Illinois, and is considered the forerunner of the grain binder. Unlike McCormick's reaper, which by then included a "self rake" to rake the cut grain off of the platform, the Marsh harvester used a moving canvas that transported the cut grain over the drive wheel and dropped it in a "bunch" just outside of the drive wheel. There it could be easily banded or bundled without first dropping to the ground. By 1880, Deering had acquired controlling interest in the firm and Deering Harvester was formed.

Competition for harvester sales was fierce, and a period of guerrilla marketing marked the so-called Harvester Wars of the mid-1880s as the many reaper makers fought for sales. Meanwhile, the major players sought relief. In 1890, McCormick, Deering, and eighteen of their competitors joined together for relief from competition and formed American Harvester Company. But the firm existed only briefly. Six of the major stockholders elected young Cyrus president and the aging Deering as chairman. American Harvester was disbanded when it was apparent there were no working plans, and neither Deering, McCormick, nor any banks were willing to finance

1858 Marsh harvester

Invented in 1858 by brothers Charles W. and William W. Marsh, Shabbona Grove, Illinois, farmers, the Marsh harvester formed the basis of the company created in 1880 that was eventually controlled by William Deering as the Deering Harvester Co. The Marsh harvester transported the cut grain over the drive wheel where it was deposited on a table, ready for binding. It was the forerunner of Deering's grain binder, which by 1885 had progressed to an all-steel twine binder.

William Deering

Cyrus H. McCormick II was president and William Deering was chairman of the board of the new International Harvester Co. organized August 12, 1902, in the boardrooms of J. P. Morgan and Company of New York. Morgan partner George W. Perkins was the third member of a ten-year voting trust that exercised the power normally voted by stockholders.

WILLIAM DEERING
1826–1913

Weber farm wagon

The new IH began to broaden its product line soon after its 1902 organization, by buying companies with well-regarded products. It bought Weber Wagon Works of Chicago, Illinois, in 1904. The Weber line was advertised as the "King of all Farm Wagons" and was made in nine regional series to suit most of the farming conditions found from the east to the west coasts of North America.

McCormick corn binder

By the late 1880s, the Deering Harvester Co. and McCormick Harvesting Co. were bumping into each other at every turn. Deering came out with a corn binder in 1894. McCormick followed shortly with its own machine beginning in 1895. Corn bound in bundles and shocked could be shucked by hand or hauled to the barn and stored for further processing with a husker and shredder. By 1897, the two companies were looking for ways to combine forces.

the deal.

McCormick Harvesting Machine sought to buy out Deering in 1897, but the two firms could not reach an agreement. The Harvester Wars continued.

Birth of International Harvester

A solution to the dilemma was worked out by George W. Perkins in the offices of financier J. P. Morgan in New York. The new International Harvester Company was formed in 1902 by combining the assets of McCormick Harvesting Machine; Deering Harvester; Plano Manufacturing Company of Plano, Illinois; Milwaukee Harvester Company of Milwaukee, Wisconsin; and Wardell, Bushnell & Glessner of Springfield, Ohio, makers of the Champion Harvester. IH was at once a huge company for the times with a capitalization of $120 million. More importantly, the com-

bined companies controlled more than 80 percent of the reaper, binder, and mower market.

The size of the operation was both a curse and a blessing. The new group provided opportunities for expansion and manufacturing efficiencies but also fostered opposition to its size. Anti-trust fever was mounting in the United States as an increasing number of mergers were underway. IH hoped it would be considered a "good" trust with positive benefits for farm customers. To keep a low profile on its financial successes, IH delayed for six years the publicity of issuing annual reports.

In 1903, IH quietly bought an old rival, the D. M. Osborne Company of Auburn, New York. As it moved to diversify, in 1904, IH added the Weber Wagon Company of Chicago, Aultman-Miller of Akron, Ohio, and the Keystone Company of Rock Falls, Illinois. The series of consolidations and acquisitions reduced competition and added new equipment to broaden lines.

To consolidate the foreign markets previously served by both McCormick and Deering, IH set up a network of foreign-based agricultural equipment factories. In 1903, IH began a plant on Deering-owned land in Hamilton, Ontario. The first overseas factory was built at Norrkoping, Sweden, in 1905. Soon there were plants in Croix, France; Neuss, Germany; and Lubertsky, Russia. International Harvester was becoming truly international in manufacturing as well as marketing.

The Hammer Falls

Anti-trust proceedings against IH haunted it from the start. In 1912, the U.S. Justice Department filed suit against IH under the Sherman Act, touching off a fifteen-year legal battle matching IH against the courts. IH was charged with monopolizing the harvester and binder markets, destroying competition with exclusive dealer contracts, creating a patent monopoly, and reaping excessive profits. To try to divert the lawsuit, Cyrus Hall McCormick II split the company in two, with International Harvester Corporation in charge of foreign trade and International Harvester Company of New Jersey in charge of the old equipment lines.

In 1914, the court ordered IH dissolved. The company appealed to the U.S. Supreme Court. In 1918, as World War I was ending, the Court told IH it could re-unite as one corporation if it sold off D. M. Osborne, Milwaukee Harvester, and Aultman-Miller.

Emerson-Brantingham bought the Osborne line from IH, but declined to buy the Osborne manufacturing plant in Auburn, New York. The Champion line was soon sold to B. F. Avery of Louisville, Kentucky, which also declined to buy the Champion plant in Springfield, Ohio. The Milwaukee line remained unsold until 1924 when Moline Plow Company of Moline, Illinois, gave it a new home. With government consent, IH retained the plants of the Osborne, Champion, and Milwaukee Harvesters and soon converted them into the manufacture of other products.

In an obvious attempt to block other makers from the market, IH had from the start maintained at least the existing McCormick and Deering, and sometimes Osborne, dealerships in towns and made equipment specifically for each of the different dealerships. Farmers could thus patronize the same dealerships as before the formation of IH and buy equipment still marked and colored as if nothing had changed. The Court now limited IH to one dealership per town, and as a result, IH dropped more than 5,000 dealers.

On the Road to a Full Line of Implements

IH was formidable competition upon its creation in 1902, and a chief competitor, Deere & Company of Moline, Illinois, instantly noted IH's spread into a lengthening list of product lines. Deere had purposely avoided direct competition with IH by staying out of the harvester business. But as the new giant pushed ahead into other markets, Deere reappraised its situation and, in 1911, began to follow the leader by consolidating its related companies and broadening its product lines by acquiring other companies. In July 1912, Deere committed to building harvesters at a new plant in Moline, Illinois, thus opening the possibility that IH would reciprocate by entering the plow business, which it did in 1919.

IH rounded out its product line in 1919 with the purchase of the Parlin & Orendorff Company of Canton, Illinois, the third-ranked plow maker in the United States. P&O made as many as 1,400 sizes and varieties of implements. It too was a proud old company with roots going back to 1842 when William Parlin, a native of Massachusetts, made his first plows at Canton. William J. Orendorff became his partner in 1852 after a massive fire leveled the Parlin shops and capital was needed for renewal and expansion.

More variety in IH plows was added later in 1919 with the purchase of the Chattanooga Plow Works of Chattanooga, Tennessee. That firm had its start with the efforts of Newell Sanders, a maker of high-quality chilled-steel plows and other farm implements used regionally.

IH now had a full line of farm implements—with one possible exception, a gasoline-powered traction engine. And it was working on that possibility as soon as the merger was formed.

McCormick grain binder
The 1923 IH catalog notes that the company was then in the process of putting its entire line under the trade name of "McCormick-Deering."

Deering grain binder
Both McCormick and Deering names and colors were preserved for many years under IH as separate identities for product names and colors as shown on these grain binders from a 1923 products catalog from IH.

Chapter 2

Power for the Prairies

The most prominent feature noted in late tractor designs is the endeavor of builders to have light and strong tractors better adapted to general work on small- and medium-sized farms than the earlier heavy designs. The trend is unmistakably toward the small- and medium-weight machine, just as the trend in automobile designing is toward the medium-weight cars of moderate price. Tractor prices have been reduced and their use is increasing in all sections of the country.
—Victor Pagé, *The Modern Gas Tractor: Its Construction, Operation, Application and Repair,* 1917

Above: **Mogul 30/60**

1917 Mogul 10/20
Left: *It's more than eighty years old and still running. Brothers Howard and Roger Schnell of Franklin Grove, Illinois, restored their father's 1917 Mogul 10/20 in 1989.*

With the dawn of the twentieth century came the dawn of the age of the gasoline farm tractor. Steam-powered engines ruled the fields, but pioneering gasoline traction engines were challenging the steamer's supremacy. With the momentum and broader scale of operations it gained from its formation in 1902, International Harvester was looking for new products to add to its line of agricultural equipment. There was an obvious addition to make—a tractor—although at the time it must have been seen as a long shot.

The concept of the gasoline farm tractor in a workable version had shown up more than ten years earlier when northern Iowa thresherman John Froehlich harnessed a one-cylinder Van Duzen gasoline engine to make a self-propelled gasoline traction engine. With it, he pulled and powered a threshing machine for a fifty-two-day harvest season in summer and fall 1892. The Froehlich machine is considered the first practical farm tractor and the first "ancestor" of the Waterloo Boy tractor from the Waterloo Gasoline Engine Company of Waterloo, Iowa, which was purchased by Deere in 1918 to found its line of two-cylinder tractors.

In 1902, in Charles City, Iowa, recent University of Wisconsin graduates Charles W. Hart and Charles H. Parr put together a two-cylinder gasoline-powered traction engine especially geared for drawbar pulling. Their second tractor was made in 1903, and two years later the Hart-Parr Company was operating the first factory in the United States devoted solely to tractor manufacturing. By 1907, it was making 200 tractors a year. Hart-Parr sales people are generally credited with coining the term "tractor" to describe what had been called a gasoline traction engine. They captured an early, but short-lived, lead as the major tractor manufacturers.

Prior to the IH merger of 1902, both McCormick and Deering engineers had dreamed of self-propelled mowers and other machines, and built crude devices aimed at that end. Both firms were working on developing gasoline engines before IH was organized. McCormick's Auto-Mower, developed by engineer Edward A. Johnston, was shown at expositions in 1900 and garnered a first prize at the Paris Exposition that year. Deering's machine of similar construction appeared at about the same time. Neither machine was

Engineer Edward A. Johnston

developed beyond the prototype stage, but they were prophetic of future developments.

A Young Engineer's Impact

Eighteen-year-old mechanical genius Edward A. Johnston first worked for McCormick starting in 1894 during the Harvester Wars. He designed mowers, binders, headers, knotters, and corn pickers, and won his first patent in 1897 at the age of twenty-two. In 1901, he moved to the Keystone Company, where he was superintendent and design engineer. When IH purchased Keystone in 1904, Johnston moved back to Chicago to work with IH. During his forty years with IH he claimed another 161 patents and was one of the guiding forces of the firm's entrance into both the truck and tractor businesses. His influence was long felt by the company.

Johnston experimented with an automobile in 1898 during his first stint at McCormick Works in Chicago. His high-wheeled passenger vehicle with

wagon styling was powered by an opposed two-cylinder, air-cooled engine of four-cycle design. The simple engine had a bore and stroke of 5.00x5.00 inches (125x125 mm) and produced 15 hp. Johnston called his creation the Auto Buggy.

In 1906, new IH president Cyrus McCormick II empowered Johnston to build a new vehicle designed for the hauling needs of farmers. It was to run at 20 miles per hour (32 km/h), haul one ton (900 kg), and climb a 25 percent grade. The first 100 production Auto Buggies made at McCormick Works sold out as the big-wheeled machines were more comfortable on the farmers' rough roads than other machines. By 1909, production was moved from Chicago to Akron, Ohio, and improved Auto Wagons replaced the Auto Buggies.

By 1910, Auto Wagons were selling at a rate of 1,300 per year, and IH was in the truck business. By 1912, the Auto Wagon was called the Motor Truck, and by 1916, the design was replaced by a new series of trucks designated as Models H, F, K, G, and L. They were powered by rugged four-cylinder engines cooled with a radiator located at the rear of the engine at the firewall. The motor from the Model G truck was later the basis of a tractor engine when market conditions directed a quick change in tractor design.

After a brief spell of making automobiles, which lasted until 1910, IH decided to concentrate on the truck market. And following his success with trucks, Johnston's new challenge was the farm tractor.

Birth of the International Tractor

With the help of an outside firm, IH engineers developed the first IH tractor by 1905. In 1889, S. S. Morton of York, Pennsylvania, built a tractor using a stationary engine and friction drive running a geared chassis. Morton's patents of 1902 and 1903 protected some features of his design. In 1904, Morton's "trucks," including the frame and gearing, were being supplied to other gas engine makers to convert their engines into tractors. Ohio Manufacturing Company of Upper Sandusky, Ohio, was using Morton's patents, and that's where IH engineers had one of their Milwaukee-made, 15-hp "Famous" stationary engines mounted on a Morton truck. IH was suddenly in the tractor business.

The 1905 tractor worked well enough to encourage IH to have Ohio Manufacturing make another fourteen tractors in 1906. More were made in 1907, and by 1908, IH was producing the friction-drive models in Akron, Ohio, and Milwaukee, as well as at Upper Sandusky. These early friction-drive tractors were apparently available in sizes of 10, 12, 15, and 20 hp. Between the start of production in 1906 and the end of the line in 1910, the three locations built about 1,060 tractors, making up nearly a third of all the tractors ever made in the United States to that date.

Type C tractor disking
Engine cooling of the early IH tractors consisted of pumping the engine's hot water over a screen and catching it in a hopper. Thus cooled by evaporation, the water was returned to the engine. Massive flywheels kept the single-cylinder engine rotating at about 250 rpm until its next power stroke. This Type C tractor proudly bears the IHC logo on the frame just behind the front wheels. Type C tractors were IH engineered and built, first at Akron, Ohio, and later at Milwaukee, Wisconsin. The Type C was built from 1909 to 1914 as a 20- and 25-hp tractor. It became the Mogul Type C and was the only Mogul model built at Milwaukee. (Photo courtesy State Historical Society of Wisconsin #Whi0.3545)

Like their counterparts from other firms, IH friction-drive tractors were monsters for the power they produced. Starting with the heavy one-cylinder stationary engines with their massive cast flywheels mounted on a riveted-steel chassis of steam-engine scale, the complete 20-hp tractor could weigh 5 tons or more (4,500 kg)—about 500 pounds (225 kg) per horsepower. The friction drive substituted for a clutch and as part of the speed reduction for the final drive. The early engines plugged along at about 250 rpm with a hit-and-miss governor that fired the engine "igniter" more frequently as revolutions dropped. The engines were cooled by an evaporative cooling system that trickled hot engine water over a wiremesh screen and into a collecting tank.

A small, 12-inch-diameter (30-cm) pulley on the engine crankshaft could be forced to contact a large, 5-foot diameter (150-cm) pulley geared to the final drive. Thus engaged, the engine propelled the machine through its gearing at about 2 miles per hour (3.2 km/h). Levers on the operator's platform let the engineer pull the engine back to make friction contact between the pulleys. The heavy engine was mounted on rollers to make it relatively easy to move into the drive position and to release it to stop forward movement. The friction drive was less than ideal, and by 1907, gear drive replaced the friction pulleys.

Types A and B Gear-Drive Tractors

More than 600 Type A gear-drive tractors were made between 1907 and 1911. They were available with 12-, 15-, or 20-hp single-cylinder engines and were as-

Mogul Type C
Powering stationary equipment by belt power was an important use of the new gas tractors. This early IH tractor was belted to a husker shredder, which made fodder and grain from corn field-harvested with a corn binder. Other belt applications included threshing machines and silage cutters. (Photo courtesy State Historical Society of Wisconsin #WHiI-11293)

sembled by Ohio Manufacturing at Upper Sandusky. Another 359 Type A tractors with 15- or 20-hp engines were made at Akron between 1909 and 1911.

A two-speed, 12-hp gear-driven Type A tractor with friction reverse was available from 1909 to 1912. Records show only sixty-five of them were made at Upper Sandusky. But in the period 1910–1917, the Akron IH works assembled 203 Type A tractors with 12- and 15-hp engines and two-speed gear drives with friction reverse.

First available in 1908, Type B 20-hp tractors were similar to the Type A but had larger rear drive wheels of 64 inches (160 cm) diameter. Type B tractors used a single axle extending through the drive wheels whereas Type A tractors used two stub axles extending from brackets on the sub frame. Otherwise they were quite similar in construction. The Type B units had gear-drive reverse and forward transmissions with but one forward speed until 1910, when the model was available with two forward speeds.

The Upper Sandusky facility of Ohio Manufacturing made 255 Type B one-speed tractors for IH from 1908 to 1912, and another 383 with the two-speed transmission from 1910 to 1918. Akron Works made forty-six one-speed Type B tractors in 1910.

Fourth-Ranked U.S. Corporation

Success with its expansion into international markets and the addition of trucks, tractors, and gas engines put IH solidly back on top again as the prime agricultural equipment maker in the United States. An investment of $28 million in that diversification helped sales nearly double to $101.2 million between 1905 and 1910. Profits soared to $16.1 million in 1910, and assets grew to $172.7 million. That placed IH fourth in size of U.S. corporations behind U.S. Steel, Standard Oil of New Jersey, and the American Tobacco Company. That financial success subjected IH to growing scrutiny from government trustbusters, farmers worried about monopoly in the farm equipment business, and journalists taking up the popular cry for reform.

IH began to experience problems doing business in several states in 1906, based on regional and local criticism of its size and power. Arkansas fined the marketing arm of IH that year because of the size of the company, effectively forcing IH to stop all marketing in that state until 1913. A similar problem arose in Kansas the same year and it was 1910 before IH resumed sales activities there. Missouri too raised objections to IH and its size. Problems in Texas took the cake: IH left Texas in 1907 and did not resume marketing there until 1919 after anti-trust charges had been settled.

Despite the threatening anti-trust problems, tractor development, manufacturing, and sales continued at an ever-increasing pace. By 1911, IH was the U.S. leader in production and sales of gasoline-powered tractors. Its lead held firm until the early 1920s when sales of Henry Ford's famous Fordson knocked IH into second place—temporarily.

Gold in Them Field Trials

Canada was the major market for big tractors as huge wheat farms spread over the prairie provinces in the early 1900s. Moldboard plows were favored to turn under the native grasses and big engines were needed to provide power for plowing and powering the big threshing machines at harvest time. Gas engines were starting to show their advantages over the steam engines for those applications. The prairies were often many miles from the coal or wood needed to fuel steam engines. Transporting water long distances for steam machines was also an added expense. Gas or kerosene tractors used a concentrated fuel, and the water used in evaporative cooling of the big gas engines was minimal compared with steam engine use. IH wanted some of the big tractor action and energetically went after it.

Field trials and competitions were one way for early tractor makers to show and publicize their machines. Winnipeg, Manitoba, held its first Agricultural Motor Competition trials beginning in 1908. IH entered competition there with 15-, 20-, and 40-hp tractors, and was encouraged when the 15-hp machine earned the silver medal in its class. IH's first large test of its early tractors came in 1909 when the firm entered eight of its machines in the Winnipeg trials in which twenty-two tractors vied for prizes. The IH 15-hp Type A won the gold medal in its class plus the overall sweepstakes with the top score. Two of its Type B 20-hp tractors also scored, one with a gold medal and the other with a bronze in their horsepower and size category.

Birth of the Mogul and Titan

Meanwhile, back in Chicago at the McCormick Works, engineer Edward Johnston was busy with IH's development of a four-wheel, two-speed tractor that would spark the famous Mogul line. First working in cramped temporary quarters and even assembling tractors in a tent, the Tractor Works got its own permanent facilities next to the McCormick Works with construction of the new plant beginning in 1909. Tractor production began there in 1911 with the Mogul 45-hp and the Mogul Jr. 25-hp tractors.

The Mogul and Titan names were significant to International up until its consent decree with the Justice Department in 1918. Since IH retained all of the McCormick and Deering dealerships in every town from its organization in 1902, it wanted separate product lines for each dealer's brand. Mogul engines and tractors were built to be sold by McCormick dealerships; Titan engines and tractors were built for sale by Deering dealerships. Titans were built in the Milwaukee Works, and Moguls were built at the Tractor Works in Chicago. Once IH was ordered by the courts to keep but one dealership in each town, the dealers became "International" dealers selling either International-branded or McCormick-Deering–branded products after 1918's anti-trust settlement.

The Mogul line was introduced in 1909. The Type C 20-hp Mogul was among the first of the IH tractor line to use company engineering throughout. In 1910, it sold more than 1,000 copies to set a new production mark for an IH model. During its production run from 1909 to 1914, the model sold 2,441 units, another company record.

Titan 18-35

Titan threshing

Above: *The steaming square cooling hopper marks this tractor as one of the Milwaukee-made Titans sold through IH Deering dealers. The enclosed cab with roll-down side curtains indicate it was made sometime after 1912. Its two-cylinder side-by-side engine was originally rated at 45 hp. It later became a 60-hp tractor. Revolutionary at the time, cylinder sleeves were replaceable, assuring it a long, productive life. The big engine was started with compressed air stored in a tank projecting from below the cooling tank. Later versions used a gasoline starting motor instead of compressed air for starting.* (Photo courtesy State Historical Society of Wisconsin #Whi-22380)

Titan 18/35

Left: *Smaller than the Titan 45 and 30/60 was the 18/35 made from 1912 to 1915. Records show about 260 of them made during that period. Engine cooling and starting was similar to the larger Titans. It too was built to be sold by the Deering dealerships.*

Late Titan 30/60

Above: *A shrouded fan-cooled cellular radiator replaced the familiar Titan cooling tank on the Titan 30/60s built from 1914 to 1917. The engine was covered by a removable steel cover instead of an engine canopy. The engine was started by the small air-cooled gasoline engine mounted behind the radiator. The 30/60 was discontinued in 1917 marking the last of the big IH tractors.* (Photo courtesy State Historical Society of Wisconsin #WHiI-14084)

Titan 12/25

Right: *First made about 1914, the Titan 12/25 was the first IH four-cylinder tractor. Its large cellular radiator with fan cooling helped end IH dependence on tanks and towers for engine cooling. Twin stacks carried exhaust gases away from the horizontal transverse engine and its operators. A narrowed front end kept the front wheels from interfering with the belt.* (Photo courtesy State Historical Society of Wisconsin #WHiI-11753)

International 15/30

Above: *Upgraded from the Titan 15/25, the International 15/30 EC Series shed its cab and twin exhaust stacks, and added a side-mounted radiator when it took on its new name on November 21, 1917, as IH scurried to brand its products under one name. More than 5,575 International 15/30s were made by the end of production in 1921. Its four-cylinder 5.25x8.00-inch (131.25x200-mm) engine turned over at up to 575 rpm. Drive chains were fully enclosed. (Photo courtesy State Historical Society of Wisconsin #WHiI-19922)*

1911 Mogul Jr. 25 hp

Left: *A total of 812 one-cylinder Mogul Jr. models with a 25-hp rating were made in Chicago from 1911 to 1913.*

Mogul 12/25

The second most popular Mogul model was the smaller 12/25 built between 1913 and 1918 in Chicago in more than 1,500 units. It featured automotive-type steering, fan-cooled radiator, steel shrouding of the entire chassis, and a two-cylinder motor turning at a then-fast 550 rpm. It began as the Mogul 10/20 of 1912–1913 of which only 85 were made. (Photo courtesy State Historical Society of Wisconsin #WHiHB5-01A)

Mogul 30/60

Completed in 1911, the Chicago Tractor Works built Mogul 45s and 30/60s for sale by McCormick dealers. The big Mogul shared little with its Titan counterparts except power specifications. The Mogul engine was a smooth-running opposed two-cylinder engine. Starting was via an air-cooled gas engine driving the main flywheel through friction contact. Engine cooling was accomplished with a vertical radiator with exhaust induced draft. Some 2,437 30/60s were made at Chicago from 1911 through 1917.

Mogul 30-60

The Type C resembled the preceding models but was different mechanically. It used the gear drive, augmented with a spring-loaded clutch, for forward transport and the friction drive for reverse. The clutch helped the operator reduce the shock of sudden power engagement that came with the earlier gear-drive Type A tractors. The Type A machine was equipped with a spring-dampened drawbar to reduce the starting shock; the Type C also used that same drawbar arrangement.

First built at Akron, Type C production was transferred to Milwaukee in 1910 and called the Mogul Type C. It was made in 20- and 25-hp versions with 862 of the 25-hp units sold from 1911 to 1914 during Milwaukee production.

There were as many as ten different Mogul models made from 1909 to 1918, each designated by horsepower rating ranging from 60 hp down to 8/16 for the smallest of the line. The 8/16 rating signified 8 drawbar hp and 16 belt hp, a style of rating that became standard in the industry.

Chicago's Mogul 45

Of the big Moguls made at Tractor Works in Chicago, the most popular was the Mogul 45 hp of which 2,437 were made between 1911 and 1917. Its two opposed cylinders held pistons with 9.50x12.00-inch (237.5x300-mm) bore and stroke. Engine governing was hit or miss at the start of production, but was changed to throttle governing soon after. Engine speed could be advanced from 330 up to 370 rpm. Enlarging the engine bore to 10.00 inches (250 mm) later made a 60-hp tractor out of the former Mogul 45 machine.

The big twin's poor starting characteristics were finally solved by a one-hp air-cooled two-cylinder starting engine. The starting engine turned over the main engine by friction contact on the face of the right flywheel. The Mogul 45 was a huge machine with drive wheels 6 feet (180 cm) in diameter with ground contact width of 2 feet (60 cm).

IH garnered more medals for its Chicago-made Mogul 45 at the 1912 trials at Winnipeg. The gas-pow-

Mogul 8/16

A new small tractor design was to sweep through the IH line beginning with the Mogul 8/16 introduced in 1914. Sales of the two-plow single-cylinder tractor soared to 14,065 by 1917 when it was replaced with the larger Mogul 10/20. Small and easy to operate, the 8/16 blazed the trail for more smaller tractors from IH. A hand-clutched belt pulley could be attached to the flywheel on the right side of the engine. This tractor is hitched to a No. 62 Oliver plow and is shown working near Ithaca, New York, on the P. T. Kelly farm. IH salesman Arthur Mabee is on the seat. (Photo courtesy State Historical Society of Wisconsin #WHiI-11796)

ered Mogul 45 was awarded the silver medal in its class, and the kerosene-burning version got the bronze medal. IH was fast developing a reputation as a tractor maker with kerosene as well as gasoline machines. Kerosene was the low-cost fuel.

Landmark Lightweight Moguls

The smaller, 25-hp Mogul Jr. had a single-cylinder engine. It was made between 1911 and 1913 with a production run of only 812 tractors. A 10/20 Mogul built in Chicago in 1912 to 1913 was limited to 85 units, while the 15/30 Mogul model saw but 527 tractors of its kind roll out the door from 1913 to 1915.

The Mogul 12/25 of 1911 vintage was a landmark tractor for IH. It shed weight in exchange for performance, used a cellular radiator with side-mounted fan, and enclosed the engine from the radiator to the

cab with yards of sheet metal. Another borrowing from the automobile was its automotive-type steering that replaced the chain-and-bolster steering of other tractors of the day. By 1916, the 12/25 even featured an exhaust muffler.

The 12/25 was powered by two 7.00x8.00-inch (175x200-mm) opposed cylinders spinning the crankshaft at 550 rpm to get more work done. This engine speed was about twice the rpm the other tractor engines were turning. Sales of the 12/25 between 1913 and 1918 reached 1,543 units, providing early proof that perhaps size alone was not the only way to build a tractor.

The Titan Model Line

The Titan was made in a comparable number of models. It was generally of the same horsepower rating

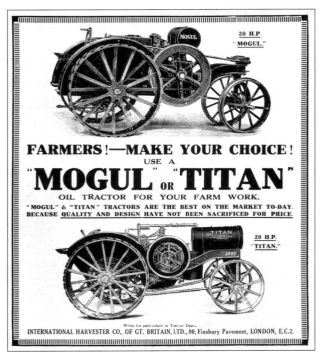

Above, top: **Mogul 10/20 identification plate**

Above, bottom: **British ad for Mogul and Titan 20-hp models**

1917 Mogul 10/20

Right: *Hopper cooling through the large stack keeps the one-cylinder engine on the Mogul 10/20 from overheating. Air intake is through the high stack. Exhaust exits through a muffler under the tractor. Open chain drive runs the left drive wheel. Its 8.50x12-inch (212.50x300-mm) cylinder and two-speed spur-gear transmission gave it power to pull a three-bottom plow under most conditions. Sales of the Mogul 10/20 were limited to 8,985 units during its 1916 to 1919 production primarily because of competition from another International tractor, the Titan 10/20.*

and weight as the comparable Mogul model, but differed in the mechanical route to those specifications. The Type D Titan Series from the Milwaukee Works was introduced in 1910, and 20-, 25-, and 45-hp tractors were made. The smallest, 20-hp Type D Titan sold only 274 units during its production run from 1910 to 1914. The 25-hp Type D Titan fared better with 1,757 tractors made and sold during the same years of production.

Larger tractors were in the works by 1910 as the Canadian trials had its impact. A 45-hp Type D debuted in 1910 as the Reliance, soon renamed a Titan. With modification, it became a 60-hp tractor before its production ended in 1915 after 1,319 were made. This model had a side-by-side twin-cylinder engine, but unlike other side-by-side twins, its crankshafts were also set side by side to provide a power stroke on every revolution. Although well balanced in most respects, the Titan twins, with both pistons, rods, and cranks changing travel directions at the same time, could impart characteristic vibrations at certain rpm settings. Power output was smooth, however, because the engine produced a power stroke every 360 degrees of crankshaft rotation.

Starting the big 9.00x14.00-inch (225x350-mm) Titan two-cylinder engine was aided by compressed air. A front-mounted gasoline engine-compressor pumped up an air reservoir to 200 psi. To turn the engine over for starting, compressed air was valved into the left cylinder propelling the engine forward until the right cylinder fired and started the engine. Similar air starting was used on large stationary engines of the day.

Only 176 Type D 30/60 Titans were made at Milwaukee from 1914 to 1917. On the 30/60, the 145-gallon-capacity (551-liter) box-shaped cooling tank was later replaced with a shrouded fan-cooled cellular radiator. The air start system was eventually replaced with a friction-drive starting motor common to the big 45-hp and 30/60 Moguls.

A smaller Type D Titan of 18/35 hp made between 1912 and 1915 added another 259 tractors to Milwaukee Works production. The 18/35 Titan used the same air start system used on the 45 and 30/60 Titans.

The Milwaukee factory also built thirty-nine Titan Convertible Road Rollers of 20 hp and fifty-one of 25 hp between 1912 and 1914. The front frame of

Above, top: **Mogul 10/20 final roller chain drive**

Mogul 10/20 tricycle front suspension pedestal
Above, bottom: *Narrow-tread front wheels "cut under" the goose neck front frame for quick turns from the worm-and-sector steering. A plow guide that ran in the furrow was attached to the projecting front axle and suspended from the triangular frame over the front wheels.*

Mogul 10/20 engine head and operator's platform

the Road Roller was extended forward and up into a gooseneck shape to undermount the wide front roller that substituted for the tractor's front wheels. The roller tractors constituted one of the firm's first steps into the construction business.

Early Four-Cylinder Titan

The Titan 12/25 set new precedents in IH tractor design. It had a transverse-mounted four-cylinder to earn its salt. Bore and stroke on the engine was 5.25x8.00 inches (131.25x200 mm). Rated horsepower was produced at 575 rpm, resulting in a faster-turning engine than most of its predecessors.

The Titan 12/25 was apparently IH's first attempt at harnessing four cylinders. It first appeared in late 1914 as the Titan 12/25 but became the Titan 15/30 as it proved its strength and became the "International" Titan 15/30 from 1917 on when IH began to rename its tractor models as they would soon be marketed by "International" dealers instead of separate McCormick and Deering dealers.

Besides the four-cylinder engine, the later Titan 15/30 also had several other features that distin-

guished it from other tractors of the day. Early models had twin exhaust pipes protruding through the cab; this changed to a single stack when the cab was removed from the tractor later in its production. An early front-facing cellular radiator cooled by a rear-mounted fan was changed to a sideways-mounted radiator cooled with a right-side-mounted fan in its later years.

The TS Series Titan 15/30 totaled only 780 units between 1914 and 1917; the TW Series was made only in 1917 to a total of 376 tractors. More popular was the EC Series Titan 15/30 started in 1918 and produced until 1922. The first 500 of the EC series wore the familiar cab, but it disappeared after that. By 1920, an air cleaner was an option. Records show 5,578 of the late-version Titan EC were manufactured. Like its more popular smaller 10/20 brother, the Titan 15/30 EC Series wore gray enamel paint with red wheels.

Smaller Mogul and Titan Tractors Succeed

In 1914, IH created a tractor design that forever reversed the direction toward larger tractors. The Mogul 8/16 was a small, simple, one-cylinder tractor built

Harvesting grain with Titan 10/20

Above: *By the end of its production run in 1922, the Titan 10/20 had sold a record 78,363 tractors, fought Ford in the tractor wars, and become a synonym for "tractor." In March 1922, IH General Manager Alexander Legge dropped the price of the popular tractor to $700 and threw in a free three-bottom P&O plow to help stem the loss of tractor sales to the $395 Fordson tractor. IH lost the battle but won the war.* (Photo courtesy State Historical Society of Wisconsin #WHiI-17837)

Titan 10/20

Right: *Simplicity was the strength of the Milwaukee-made Titan 10/20 first seen in 1915. Its two side-by-side 6.50x8-inch (162.50x200-mm) cylinders traveled together in the fashion of earlier Titans, giving it a power stroke every revolution and the need for extra counterweighting to tame its fore-and-aft vibrations. The engine turned at 500 rpm, until 1919 when it was goosed up to 575 rpm. Cooling was by thermosiphon from the engine to the front-mounted tank. Speeds of 2¼ and 2⅞ mph (3.6 and 4.6 km/h) forward and 2⅞ (4.6 km/h) in reverse fitted it to its role in the field: primary and secondary tillage. The Titan 10/20 frame and front steering followed that used on the Mogul 10/20.* (Photo courtesy State Historical Society of Wisconsin #WHiI-19920)

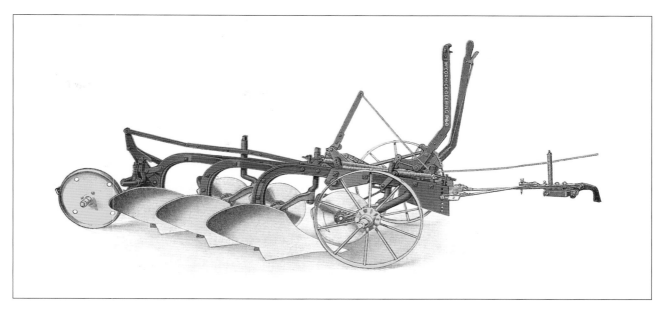

Tractor plow
Plows similar to this McCormick-Deering three-bottom tractor plow were part of a sales device used by IH beginning in 1922 to help sell Titan 10/20 tractors. The plows were given to farmers who bought new IH Titan 10/20 tractors. IH had bought the Canton, Illinois, Parlin & Orendorff plow company in 1919.

to replace horses rather than steam engines on North American farms. Starting with but twenty tractors built in 1914, its popularity soared. In 1915, the Tractor Works built 5,111; in 1916, production jumped to 8,269; and in 1917, another 665 tractors left the factory—even though the model's replacement was already in production.

The similar, but more powerful Mogul 10/20 came out in 1916. Its sales of 8,985 between 1916 and 1919 were reined in only by a competitor within the IH family. That machine was the Milwaukee-made Titan 10/20, a machine of such popularity that the name "Titan" became synonymous with "tractor" to people of the era.

True to its Titan roots, the 10/20 was powered with a two-cylinder side-by-side engine with a front-mounted cylindrical tank for its thermosiphon cooling. Its two cylinders featured bore and stroke of 6.50x8.00 inches (162.5x200 mm), giving it power to pull three plows at about 2¼ mph (3.6 km/h). Top speed in second gear was 2⅞ mph (4.6 km/h); reverse also peaked at 2⅞ mph (4.6 km/h).

In terms of size and scale the Titan 10/20 bore little resemblance to its larger kin. Weight had been trimmed to 5,700 lb (2,565 kg) to give it 285 lb (128.25 kg) per horsepower. Its drawbar had adjustments so

it could be accurately set to pull plows and a variety of drawn implements. Painted gray with red wheels, the Titan 10/20 made an attractive small package.

Sales of the Titan 10/20 were modest at 2,246 in its first full year of production in 1916. IH received proof of the need for small tractors as sales quadrupled to 9,044 in 1917, nearly doubled in 1918 to 17,675, stabilized at 17,234 in 1919, rose to 21,503 in 1920, then began to fall in 1921 to 7,729, and skidded to 2,925 sales in 1921, the model's last year of production, as even smaller tractors began to make their mark. The total production run of the Titan 10/20 was an amazing 78,363 units between 1916 and 1922. The production figure was even more fantastic considering that all of the IH plants combined had built only 76,310 tractors of all other models from 1905 to 1922. The era of the lightweight tractor had dawned and IH was leading the way.

Chapter 3

The Tractor War

It should be inspiring to the imagination of future gas-tractor Napoleons to note that our "inefficient underpowered farms"—to quote the present secretary of agriculture and several captains of industry— now employ approximately 24,000,000 mechanical horse power.
—Barton W. Currie, *The Tractor*, 1916

Above: **McCormick-Deering 10/20 from the IH dealers catalog of 1923**

1919 International 8/16
Left: *Four inline cylinders equipped with overhead valves powered the new 8/16 IH kerosene tractor of 1917.*

Bad news was looming on the horizon. A new lightweight competitor from Henry Ford, the Fordson tractor, debuted in 1917 and soon dominated North American tractor sales. The Fordson naturally impacted IH as well as other tractor makers. By 1921, a post–World War I recession also hung over the heads of farmers, which cast gloom on tractor sales for the nearly 200 companies then in the business. Many tractor makers eventually folded during the era of the Tractor War.

The Fordson was a "lightweight" only in terms of its size. It weighed about 2,700 lb (1,215 kg), claimed 20 hp from an inline four-cylinder engine, had an integral frame, and pulled a two-bottom plow at 3 mph (4.8 km/h).

Henry Ford had already put rural America on the road with his Model T, and the Fordson promised similar results on the farm. In 1917, Ford made a deal with the British government for 6,000 Fordsons to help produce food in Great Britain for the war effort, and Canada ordered another 1,000 tractors. Ford would enter the U.S. market in 1918, initially selling the Fordson only through government agencies. With an introductory price of $750, the tractor was an immediate hit. Most tractor makers underestimated its impact until its U.S. sales topped 34,000 in 1918, its first year on the market in the United States. In 1919, Ford made 54,000 Fordsons compared with a total of 26,933 tractors from IH.

In early 1922, Henry Ford cut the price of the Fordson to a new low of $395, considerably below its cost of production. In 1923, Ford sold an amazing number of tractors, some 100,000 Fordsons, while IH made only 12,206 tractors. The score? IH had 9 percent to Ford's 76 percent of the 131,908 tractors made in the United States that year. Meanwhile, other tractor makers were dropping like flies as few could compete in an agricultural depression with a mass-produced Fordson priced at under $400. From a high of 186 U.S. tractor manufacturers in 1921, the ranks were cut in half to 93 makers in 1923, and to nearly half again, or 51 surviving makers, in 1928.

For IH's tractor business, it was a situation of life or death. When asked what IH was going to do about Ford's price cut, the legendary and highly regarded IH General Manager Alexander Legge is said to have answered, "Do? Why damn it all, meet him, of course! We're going to stay in the tractor business. Yes, cut $230. Both models. Yes, both. And, say, listen, make it good! We'll throw in a plow as well!" The Tractor War was thus joined.

Legge dropped prices in February 1922 to a new IH low. Prices were cut on the popular Titan 10/20 from an already low $900 in 1921 down to a new low of $700, and on the International 8/16 from $1,000 to $670. Legge then sweetened the deal with a free three-bottom Little Genius tractor plow with a 10/20 sale and a two-bottom Little Genius tractor plow with an 8/16 sale. IH dealers and fieldmen also began demonstrating IH rigs against the Fordson whenever they heard of a Fordson sale about to happen in their territory. The Tractor War was getting serious.

The real winner of the Tractor War was the tractor buyer. Farmers got better products with more features, utility, and durability. Manufacturers won too in that they learned to mass produce quality machines at lower cost. The Tractor War also spurred IH to develop a new line of modern standard tractors, tractors so good they eventually sent the Fordson packing and put IH back on top.

Fours for Farms

The competitive situation between IH and Ford got worse before it got better. In 1916, International moved quickly to catch up with the need for lightweight four-cylinder tractors. Borrowing from its truck technology, IH engineers adapted existing automotive-style engine designs to tractors. It needed to leave behind some of its popular two-cylinder designs to arrive at the right time with the right machine. It missed its mark, but only its timing was off.

IH engineers developed an advanced machine right for its time when first proposed, but by the time it was produced, developing technology both inside and outside of IH left it in the dust. First seen in 1916 as the 8/16 Mogul, the new tractor became the International 8/16 when production began in 1917, the same year the Fordson went to England to help with the war effort.

The International 8/16 had an almost streamlined look. Its rounded sheet-metal hood tapered upward from the front to a radiator mounted at the rear of the engine above the flywheel. Under that hood was a rugged four-cylinder inline valve-in-head engine with the same 4.00x5.00-inch (100x125-mm) bore and stroke of the Model G International truck engine.

1919 International 8/16

Above: *The 8/16 was built by the Chicago Tractor Works and was first called a Mogul, for sale by McCormick dealers. It was painted green like the other Mogul machines. This 1919 VB Series 8/16 was restored by owner Merrill Sheets of Delaware, Ohio. It is serial number VB5345. In mid-1919, the VB Series was replaced by the HC Series, which had a complete crankcase and was painted gray with red wheels like the other Internationals.*

Limits on production

Left: *From 1917 to 1922, some 33,138 International 8/16s were made, not nearly enough to stem the stream of Fordsons that swelled to 62,000 tractors in 1922 alone. Engineering problems and shortages of materials during World War I were blamed for keeping numbers down. But the 8/16 laid important groundwork in developing more advanced tractors. IH's next three models were stunners.*

Tractor cousin

Above: *With its radiator on the firewall, the engine compartment was easy to access on the International Model F truck. It was built from 1916 to 1923. On June 14, 1916, a Model F International was the first truck to climb Pike's Peak in Colorado. The Model F engine had a bore and stroke of 3.50x5.25 inches (87.5x131.25 mm). Solid rubber tires were standard. Pneumatic tires were an option.*

Truck and tractor cousins

Right: *IH engineers based the engine of their 8/16 tractor on their Model G truck's 4x5-inch (100x125-mm) four-cylinder engine. Both engines also turned at 1,000 rpm. The International 8/16 tractor and this Model F International tank truck share the sloping hood with the radiator placed at the rear of the engine compartment above the flywheel.*

Both the truck and tractor engines were designed to operate at 1,000 rpm.

The trucks also used a similar sloping hood and the fan-cooled radiator mounted at the rear of the engine on the firewall. Some observers say the rear-mounting of the truck radiators was to save them from damage caused by other trucks backing into them at crowded shipping docks. That feature at least reduced the truck's hood area for better forward visibility and gave the International trucks their own distinctive streamlined look.

The 1917 tractor was IH's first with an inline four-cylinder engine. It had replaceable sleeves for easy engine servicing. The 8/16 was also equipped with au-

tomotive-type steering. These and other features made the two-plow machine about as modern a tractor as could then be imagined—except, perhaps, for its nemesis the Fordson, and some new designs then forming in the minds of IH engineers.

The 8/16 used an Ensign JK carburetor to enable it to run on gasoline or kerosene, a high-tension magneto with impulse coupling for easy starting, multiple-disc dry clutch, and a three-speed sliding-gear transmission. Its gears gave it ground speeds of 1¾, 2½, and 4 mph (2.8, 4, and 6.4 km/h). Reverse was 2⅓ mph (3.7 km/h). About the only features that harked back to earlier tractor design was its channel-frame construction and the final drive via a roller chain running to the drive-wheel sprocket.

Although still a heavy tractor, weight had been pared down to about 3,300 lb (1,485 kg), or just over 205 lb (92 kg) per horsepower. It was definite progress in the power-to-weight ratio.

PTO Pioneer

Another advanced feature of the 8/16 was its role in giving agriculture a new power source for trailed implements, the power take-off or PTO. First envisioned as early as 1880, the first practical external powershaft capable of driving towed farm implements was added to the International 8/16 in 1919 through the efforts of IH engineer Bert Benjamin. Benjamin's vision and steadfast commitment to a cause in which he believed was to serve IH well in later years. His inspiration and driving force behind many more future IH developments would help put the company back in the driver's seat in the competitive tractor and implement business.

Three series of the International 8/16 were produced from 1917 to 1922, with each new series designated after a major refinement or redesign to cure or improve on engineering problems. The initial VB Series was produced from 1917 to 1919. The improved HC Series with a different crankcase design and a water-bath air cleaner started in 1919, and the final, IC Series began in 1922 as production was winding down. The IC Series supported its fuel tank on a bracket pressed from sheet steel that extended down to the frame, giving the tractor a more finished look. The tractors were initially painted a light green but were changed to gray with red wheels with the HC Series starting in mid-1919.

1923 McCormick-Deering 15/30 features and specifications

Only 38 units were made in 1917, 3,162 in 1918, 7,571 in 1919, and 5,845 in 1920. Production peaked at 9,013 tractors in 1921, and a respectable 7,506 units were made in 1922. Total production for the six-year run of the 8/16 only came to 33,138 tractors. In comparison, Ford made 62,000 Fordsons in 1922 alone for a 63 percent share of the total 1922 U.S. tractor production of 98,724 tractors. IH made 11,781 tractors that year for its 12 percent share of the total. More than half—nearly 64 percent—of IH production in 1922 was its little four-cylinder International 8/16.

Supply Problems

Looking back at the 8/16's lack of success in holding back the Fordson, Cyrus McCormick III cast blame on engineering problems and diversion of factory effort to war production in 1918 as the main factors that kept 8/16 production low. The 8/16 was often in short supply and could probably have sold more had tractors been available.

But despite its lack of success in the sales arena,

1928 McCormick-Deering 10/20

This IH model played a prime role in competing with the Fordson tractor for market share in America. After its introduction in 1923, the two-plow tractor sold more than 215,000 units until production ended in 1938. The three-plow 15/30 was produced from 1921 to 1934 with more than 156,000 made.

the little tractor got IH rolling with modern lightweight tractors. There were already some blockbuster new IH tractor designs about to hit production when the 8/16 bowed out. IH archive photographs suggests the Tractor Works pioneered its new continuous production line (most likely patterned after the Ford assembly line) using the 8/16 tractor as a warm-up for future tractor mass production and assembly.

New Tractors to the Front Line

The tide of battle in the Tractor War was about to turn in 1921 when IH announced a completely new and modern tractor, the McCormick-Deering 15/30. The 15/30 was designed by the company from the

ground up not only to compete with the Fordson, but to "plow it under" with superior power, productive features, and long-lasting quality construction. It succeeded in all respects and was produced until about 1932 with more than 156,000 tractors made.

Following close behind the 15/30 was a smaller sibling, the McCormick-Deering 10/20, announced in 1923. Quite similar in all respects but in a smaller size, the 10/20 was to become the more popular of the two machines. Its production passed 215,000 units in its fifteen-year production run.

Key features of the two tractors were their single-piece cast-iron "bathtub" frames running from the front axle to the rear axle. An all-enclosed final drive-

McCormick-Deering 10/20 operator platform
Above: *The operator was protected by fenders. Many 10/20s were sold on rubber tires in 1930s.*

1928 McCormick-Deering 10/20
Right: *A cast frame holding the engine, clutch, transmission, and final gear drive in constant perfect alignment was a feature of the rugged standard tractor IH introduced in 1923. A tall air intake and an air cleaner were early signs the tractor was made to last. A larger sibling was the 15/30, introduced in 1921. Clem Seivert of Granger, Iowa, restored this sparkling 10/20.*

train, or gear drive, was fully sealed for protection from dust and dirt with all gears running in oil. The tractors' rugged four-cylinder valve-in-head engines had beefy crankshafts running on ball bearing front and rear mains. The extra strength of the crankshafts eliminated the need for a center main bearing. Splash-and-pressure engine lubrication gave the tractor series a long and dependable life. A water-bath air cleaner with a high intake position provided the engines with clean air to breath. Roller and ball bearings were used extensively elsewhere in the tractor.

The McCormick-Deering 15/30 weighed 6,000 lb (2,700 kg), had an 85-inch (212.5-cm) wheelbase, and could turn in a 30-foot (9-meter) circle. Its rear drive wheels were 54 inches (135 cm) in diameter with a one-foot (30-cm) face, and the front wheels were 34

inches (85 cm) tall with a 6-inch (15-cm) face.

The upright, inline four-cylinder engine of the 15/30 measured 4.50x6.00 inches (112.5x150 mm) bore and stroke and was governed at 1,000 rpm with a fly-ball throttle governor. The 15/30's Nebraska test in August 1922 rated it at 15.35 drawbar and 32.86 belt hp. The 15/30 came equipped with the governor, rear wheel fenders, wide operator's platform, belt pulley, adjustable drawbar, angle lugs, high-tension magneto, a handy brake, and radiator curtain, all for the price of $1,250. Power take-off was available, but optional.

The 15/30 was considered a three-plow tractor but power was increased in 1929 with an increase in the bore to 4.75 inches (118.75 mm) and an rpm boost to 1,050. That increased output to 22/36 hp and gave it power to pull four plows. Its horsepower-to-weight ratio thus moved from 200 lb (90 kg) per horsepower to 167 lb (75 kg) per horsepower. Although briefly called the 22/36, it was still officially the 15/30.

In contrast, the McCormick-Deering 10/20 was much lighter at 3,700 lb (1,665 kg), was shorter with a 78-inch (1,195-cm) wheelbase, and also turned in a 30-foot (9-meter) circle. Its rear drive wheels had a 42-inch (105-cm) diameter with a face width of 12 inches (30 cm). Front wheels were 30 inches (75 cm) in diameter with faces of 4.5 inches (11.25 cm).

Engine bore and stroke of the 10/20 was 4.25x5.00 inches (106.25x125 mm) and it too was governed at 1,000 rpm. The 10/20 was a two-plow tractor and featured 185 lb (83 kg) of weight per horsepower. The 10/20 came with the same standard equipment and options as the 15/30.

Industrial Model 20 and 30

Model 20 McCormick-Deerings produced from 1923 through 1948 were modified industrial tractors based on the 10/20 design. A total of 17,918 industrial Model 20s were built from 1923 through 1940. Some Model 20 industrial tractors were equipped with dual pneumatic truck tires as early as 1927. The Model 30 built from 1930 through 1932 in numbers totaling only 532, is not the W-30, but a short-lived industrial version of the 15/30.

Looking to the Future

The two new tractors from IH pulled the company steadily toward a more favorable share of the U.S. trac-

Farming advice

As one its marketing efforts, IH established its own Extension Department to promote education for farmers in the use of modern farming methods. Included was the offering of educational booklets similar to this one on the need for lime on farm soils. The company's extension department had about 100 titles "on practically all subjects affecting the farm, the farm home and the community." IH urged its dealers to make use of the booklets, charts, lantern slides, and motion pictures in developing community short courses on production and home topics.

tor market. IH's share climbed from its low of 9 percent in 1923 to 16 percent in 1924, 20 percent in 1925, 29 percent in 1926, and to a commanding lead of 55 percent of the entire market in 1928. By then there were only fifty-one surviving tractor makers, and some of them were about to be merged into even fewer survivors due to unfolding economic events.

The scene in many International showrooms in 1923 showed just how fast change had occurred in the tractor business. Still waiting for buyers in some

Red Babies

Times were tough for all sectors of agriculture in the early 1920s, including IH and its farm equipment dealers. Faced with a surplus of light-truck components, IH General Manager Alexander Legge, in another of his inspired decisions, had the parts assembled into light trucks that were then sold at a discount to McCormick-Deering dealers.

The Model S trucks were painted an attention-grabbing bright red. As they rambled over the countryside making deliveries and service calls, they were nicknamed "Red Babies." Legge thus helped the firm's dealers and the company gain recognition and stature when they needed it most.

The IH 1923 products catalog pointed out to McCormick-Deering dealers the advantages of the little red trucks: "The Red Baby of the McCormick-Deering dealer works in the interests of the farmer, upholding the Harvester Company's long established reputation as the chief servant of Agriculture in the invention of time and labor-saving farm machines and power equipment. By means of the Red Baby, the McCormick-Deering dealer is building his own business upon the solid foundation of this reputation and bringing his customers into that closer relationship which insures a permanent and worthwhile success."

What dealer could resist such an appeal? The Model S (for speed) had pneumatic tires with whitewalls, and could cruise down country lanes at a break-neck 30 mph (48 km/h) at a time when its older International heavy-hauling relatives were grinding along on solid rubber tires at half that speed. Electric lights, starter, and even an electric horn were standard on the Model S. In many different configura-tions the Model S truck soon became a favorite of farmers.

Was the success and the precedent set by the color of the little red truck the reason IH forsook gray and in 1936 chose red as the color of its tractors?

International Red Baby literature
The Red Babies were a "bright red emblem of service" for dealers.

stores were unsold chain-drive two-cylinder Titan 10/20s and four-cylinder Mogul 15/30s with their de-signs and construction dating to the very start of the tractor business. Side by side were parked the new McCormick-Deering 15/30s and 10/20s showing IH's future in the tractor business. That future was only about a year away, and it was a future that would revo-lutionize the farm tractor.

Chapter 4

To Farm All

It's homely as the devil, but if you don't want to buy one you'd better stay off the seat.
—Texas farmer after using an experimental Farmall, 1923

Above: **1924 Farmall**

1928 Farmall
Left: *By 1932, at least nine out of ten row-crop tractors at work were Farmalls.*

From an unlikely beginning evolved a machine that was destined to set new levels in tractor usefulness and human productivity. That unlikely beginning was IH's top-heavy, ungainly, short-lived failure, the 1917–1920 Motor Cultivator. The tractor that was destined to revolutionize farming was the famous Farmall.

Pursuing what is now called the two-tractor approach, IH and many of its competitors from 1915 to 1918 offered farmers a second machine designed specifically to cultivate row crops, thus replacing horses and mules still kept to do that work. Manufacturers saw opportunities in selling their cultivating tractors to that end. Farmers, on the other hand, disliked the thought of having to buy a separate machine that could be used only a few months a year for but one useful application. So the farmers held onto their horses, saving them primarily for crop cultivation.

Row-crop cultivation was as much an art as a science. Farmers took pride in doing it well. Control of crop-choking weeds in corn required a three-pass technique. The first cultivation ran down the rows in the direction of planting. The second pass was across the rows or "cross" cultivation in the checkrow created by hill planting at the width of the row. Then corn was "laid by" with a third and final cultivation, again down the planted rows, at about the time the corn leaves were meeting between the rows.

It was slow, tedious work requiring a team of two horses and a man for a single-row cultivator, or three horses and a man for a two-row cultivator. Reins in hand, the operator also had to steer the cultivator with foot pedals to keep the blades or shovels centered over the rows. Otherwise, the farmer could plow out carefully tended crops.

Cultivation was done at one of the hottest times of the year, and working every day in the heat was exhausting and draining on the team. Unless they were cooled down by resting at row ends, horses could literally die in the harness. Mules were favored over horses for crop cultivation in the southern United States because, by some internal instinct for self-preservation, the mules balked before they overheated.

There was indeed a need for mechanizing row-crop cultivation. Unfortunately, then-current tractor designs were not suited to the task.

Motor Cultivator steering
The rear steering mechanism locked into a centered position for cultivation. Cultivator guidance was by foot-pedal steering of the two front wheels. A small belt pulley was added to gain more farm uses of the motor during the months the cultivator was not needed in the cornfields.

Motor Cultivator controls
The Motor Cultivator operator sat over the two rows and steered the cultivator down the rows with foot pedals. At row ends, the operator cranked rapidly on the wheel in his or her lap to turn the engine and drive wheels enough to turn the machine around and head down the next pair of rows.

A Better Way?

In 1917, IH senior engineer Edward A. Johnston and engineer Carl W. Mott patented a unique cultivating tractor designed to join other farm implement makers in replacing the millions of horses and mules used for row-crop cultivation on farms. The machine was basically a two-row cultivator to which a rear motor drive unit was attached. Power was from a high-mounted four-cylinder LeRoi engine of 12 hp. It pushed the two-wheeled cultivator through a pedestal-mounted drive, geared to two narrow-spaced rear drive wheels. The machine was, in effect, a backward-traveling tricycle.

IH began offering its Motor Cultivator to farmers in 1917, and in that year one hundred were built and thirty-one were sold. All thirty-one were promptly recalled to the factory to fix major deficiencies.

In 1918, heavy cast-iron wheels replaced the rim-and-spoke cultivator wheels in an attempt to fix the top-heavy Motor Cultivator's tendency to roll over. The engine's high location put the machine's center of gravity too high, and the heavy wheels only slightly helped its proclivity to topple on even modest slopes.

On row ends rapid cranking of the steering wheel was needed to quickly turn the unit around and into the new pair of rows. Once lined up on the row, the drive unit was locked into a centered position and the operator did the careful down-the-row steering with foot pedals, much like the steering needed with a horse-drawn cultivator. Some farmers who tried the machine liked it. Others did not.

An estimated three hundred Motor Cultivators were built for the 1918 marketing year. Some were delivered too late for the early summer cultivating season, and by the end of the year as many as half were left unsold. A few more sold in 1919, and sixty-two were carried into 1920. After a close-out price, the last one sold in July 1920. Records show that it was the prospect of a price increase to a non-competitive level that finally killed the Motor Cultivator design.

Dawn of the Farm-All Concept

The failure of the little Motor Cultivator did not dampen the promise of one tractor powering some, if not all, of the farm equipment needed on the aver-age farm, or at least of a machine that could replace animal power in row-crop cultivation. The IH Experimental Department ended up with some of the failed Motor Cultivators to use for its own purposes. Photographs in the IH archives, dated between 1919 and 1920, show the machines being used as test-beds for front-mounted binders, plows, corn planters, sweep rakes, and other equipment. At one point late in the ongoing experiments, the narrow-spaced rear drive wheels were replaced with a single crawler track.

Much of the story of the gradual evolution of the new row-crop tractor unfolds in the IH Advertising Department's chronicle "Farmall Tractor History," assembled in the early 1930s by C. W. Gray and maintained in the IH archives in Madison, Wisconsin.

By November 11, 1919, the Engineering Department had discarded the "Motor Cultivator" term and was calling its proposed all-purpose machine the "Farm-All."

A major experimenter with the attachments for the ungainly machine was the same Bert R. Benjamin who had successfully created the rear power take-off for the International 8/16. Benjamin had also developed a PTO-driven binder to take advantage of that major development in power transmission. As Superintendent of Experiments at the McCormick Works in Chicago, Benjamin had long-envisioned one farm power unit driving attached implements to handle all of a farm's power needs. It was toward this goal that he was developing add-on implements for the old Motor Cultivator.

More combinations were tried by the Experimental Department as 1920 progressed. By that time, the experimental power unit was being powered through the front wheels (where the cultivator wheels had been) and steered with a single rear wheel, still running below the transverse-mounted rear engine. The unit was reversible and could be operated in either direction.

Farm-All evolution continued into 1920, and other mounted equipment was tried on the rig. Those included the absolutely essential cultivator, a grain header, corn picker, sweep rake, side delivery rake, and corn binder. By late 1920, the archive photos show a late version with the engine finally mounted inline on the tractor's channel frame. The prototype was

Motor Cultivator engine

Above: *Power came from a pedestal-mounted four-cylinder LeRoi 12-hp engine pushing the cultivator through closely spaced dual wheels at the rear of the cultivator. The engine and the drive mechanism all swiveled as the machine turned.*

1918 IH Motor Cultivator

Left: *Awkward in its appearance and operation, the 1918 two-row Motor Cultivator held within its ungainly lines the promise of a machine that could revolutionize the use of power in agriculture. A machine that could till, plant, cultivate, and harvest—a machine that could farm all. This "ugly duckling," taken off the market when it failed as a power cultivator, became the nucleus of a long-term experimental effort at IH that resulted in the famous Farmall row-crop tractor. Tractor collector Wes Stratman of Pueblo, Colorado, restored this historic machine, which was photographed while on loan to the Tractor Test Museum at the University of Nebraska at Lincoln.*

1920 Farm-All prototype
By 1919, IH engineers were referring to their project tractor as the "Farm-All." This 1920 prototype still carried a transverse-mounted engine over the rear wheel that drove the machine through its wide front wheels and pushed the implement in front as had the old Motor Cultivator. Up front is a four-row corn planter. Steering was through the fork-mounted rear wheel, which carried a gear sector turned by a worm gear. (Photo courtesy State Historical Society of Wisconsin #WhiI-21958)

starting to take on its now-familiar shape.

In 1921, work continued, but with an interesting twist. In a letter dated May 28, 1921, Benjamin prophetically described his concept of the Farm-All to IH General Manager Alexander Legge, "If we take a Fordson tractor, which is said to be a satisfactory plowing rig, combine the two front wheels into one so that it will go between the rows, raise the rear axle, and set the wheels out to straddle the rows, we will then have combined, first, the same plowing outfit, second, a cultivator such as you saw in Hinsdale." (Benjamin had earlier successfully demonstrated a front-mounted cultivator in Hinsdale, Illinois, on the then-current Farm-All prototype.) And then came his closing arguments, "This can be made and sold to the farmer for $700. No two separate machines of the same plowing power and cultivating plower could be sold for less than $1,200."

Benjamin further noted that the farmer was looking for such a tractor, that it had a good chance of taking 80 percent of the market, and that IH should beat Ford to developing such a tractor. Benjamin apparently used the Fordson to illustrate his point because by then the Fordson was eating away at the historic IH tractor production lead and was thus well known and feared by all.

In 1922, twenty of the reversible experimental Farm-All tractors were built and shipped for field trials starting in April and continuing into May. They were numbered Q-203 through Q-222. They were put to use on farms in Illinois, Missouri, Iowa, Nebraska, Indiana, and Wisconsin. Conclusions reached from the 1922 field trials were used to build a better version for additional testing in 1923; the new prototype was lighter in weight and had one-directional travel. By mid-summer 1922, the new version was starting to take form. Most of the reversible 1922 Farm-Alls were scrapped.

A front-mounted cultivator was now favored with its placement just to the rear of the axles of the tricycle front wheel. This, and some other developing steering features, would help the cultivator to "dodge" quickly, especially when cross-cultivating checkrowed corn. The placement of hills of corn in checkrow planting could vary by nearly one foot (30 cm) if the planter wire was not kept uniformly taut. That meant the cultivator had to be quickly dodged to line it up with the out-of-line hills of corn.

A Hard Sell

Vocal Farm-All proponent Benjamin began an ongoing campaign of cost comparison between farm use of a Farm-All tractor and competing tractors with the need to still use horses and mules for cultivation. With the results of his tests, Benjamin began to convert one by one a skeptical IH management that his concept had merit and that it would make money for the farmer compared with then-current farm production

1922 Farm-All prototype
A well-known shape began to appear in this 1922 Farm-All prototype. The engine is mounted inline on a channel frame. The drive wheels were geared to increase under-axle crop clearance. Tricycle steering was through the front wheel. This machine was still reversible by changing the position of the operator's seat; that feature provided the opportunity for tractor-mounting of many more types of implements. Twenty units of this 1922 configuration were made and tested beginning in April 1922, on farms in Illinois, Missouri, Iowa, Nebraska, Indiana, and Wisconsin. They were scrapped after testing. (Photo courtesy State Historical Society of Wisconsin #WhiGP-2146)

methods requiring both horse and tractor power.

But Benjamin faced tough going to win overall approval for such a radical machine. The main objections centered on the failure of the Motor Cultivator, the Farm-All's "spiderly" look, as it was called in one report, and the desire to avoid building a machine that would compete with the soon-to-be-announced McCormick-Deering 10/20 tractor.

By now the skeptics within IH were slowly leaning toward Benjamin's views but needed to see an actual working Farm-All of the type proposed. Previous engineering versions of the Farm-All had changed so often that even the Farm-All proponents were confused as to its current configuration. After many committee meetings and reams of correspondence, the tractor was to be further refined into a lightweight version of about 3,229 lb (1,453 kg) powered with a four-cylinder 3.75x5.00-inch (93.75x125-mm) bore-and-stroke engine operating at about 1,200 rpm.

On February 23, 1923, the executive committee agreed to authorize the production of no more than twenty-five "new-type" Farm-Alls. Twenty-six were built and quickly shipped to farms for a real field trial. General reaction to the 1923 two-plow row-crop tractor was favorable.

Modifications were made to strengthen the rear axle and drawbar, change the frame to tubular steel, and fix some other flaws. The outlook looked bright for the new type of tractor but it was not yet out of the woods. The new McCormick-Deering 10/20 and 15/30 had tractor production all tied up.

Farm-All production was finally authorized for 1924 for a production run of 200 of the latest version; 205 were eventually produced. Reports from the field were good as the operation of the tractors was tracked. But IH put the new tractor on the market with no fanfare, still fearing that it would kill the McCormick-Deering 10/20. Initial advertising of the Farm-All was limited, if non-existent.

Unique, Practical Design

Unique to the Farmall was its high-standing, crop-clearing tricycle configuration. Its patented cultivator guidance was connected to the steering system to shift cultivator gangs quickly, and cable-actuated steering brakes facilitated short turns into the next pair of rows. The belt pulley and standard PTO added to the overall utility of the Farmall.

IH was really onto something with its practical two-plow general-purpose tractor. It could cultivate accurately and then change its implements for the next farm task. Its specialized attachments soon expanded its utility and cost-saving for farmers. A four-row cultivator was added as well as a rear-mounted mower, middlebusters, planters, and in 1931, the No. 20 mounted two-row corn picker, another contribution of Benjamin's concept of integrating implements with the tractor. The No. 20 corn picker was a

1923 Farm-All prototype

At the Tractor Works in Chicago in April 1923, a new and lighter machine was showing its final familiar shape. The new Farm-All traveled in one direction only. A front-mounted cultivator was adopted and connected to the steering for "quick dodge" movement for cross cultivating checkrowed crops. The front pedestal was later strengthened with a large casting and the steering gears improved. (Photo courtesy State Historical Society of Wisconsin #WhiGP-2702)

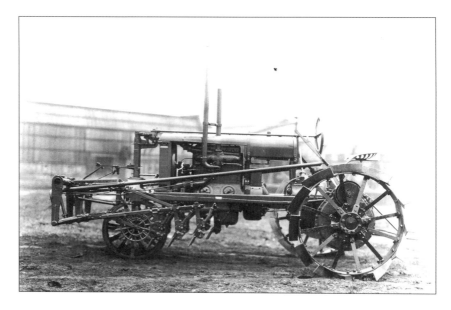

Early Farmall cultivating cotton

The Farmall became a success in Texas cotton country where several of the prototypes were initially tested. This early production Farmall was cultivating emerging cotton when this photo was taken in spring 1928. The tractor was then in its third season of use by G. V. Walker of Corpus Christi, Texas. At the insistence of cotton growers, IH was soon producing four-row planters and cultivators for the Farmall, thus nearly doubling the tractor's productivity. Note the mules working in the background. (Photo courtesy State Historical Society of Wisconsin #WhiI-37209)

Farmall laying-by corn

This June 1931 photo shows John A. Hanna of Ankeny, Iowa, cultivating checkrowed corn for its lay-by (last) cultivation. Notes with the original photo say Hanna could cultivate 20 acres (8 hectares) per day compared with the 6–8 acres (2.4–3.2 hectares) per day his father could once cultivate with horses. Like they had earlier done in cotton country, Corn Belt farmers embraced the Farmall. (Photo courtesy State Historical Society of Wisconsin #WhiI-1254-U)

Above: **1927 Farmall ad**

popular Corn Belt implement and was replaced in 1937 with improved versions.

Launch of the Farmall

Although its engineers had dubbed it the Farm-All back in 1919, official recognition of the name was to come some five years later. On July 17, 1923, the revised name "Farmall" was registered as an IH trademark. The Farmall name became official when it was authorized by the IH Naming Committee on February 5, 1924. By that time, the tractor had already entered limited production.

In November 1924, the price of the Farmall was set at $950. The cultivator attachment was $88.50, mower attachment $55, middlebreaker attachment $25 (less the middlebreaker), and a corn planter hitch $6.25. Other options included fenders for $15.

In 1925, Farmall production nudged up to a modest 838 Farmalls. In spring 1926, the new model was finally given some prominence in the IH line with a cover story in the IH *Tractor Farming* magazine that announced the firm's "new" machine would now be supplied to any section of the country. The pace of

sales that year quickened to 4,430 tractors.

In 1926, the Farmall got its own factory. The Moline Plow Company, makers of the early two-wheel general-purpose Moline Universal tractor, ran into financial problems in 1924 and stopped production of the Universal in April that year. When the firm's vacant Rock Island, Illinois, tractor plant was put on the market, IH bought it and converted the factory into the Farmall Works. Farmall production began there in 1926.

By 1927, Farmall sales more than doubled to 9,502. The popularity of the Farmall soared in 1928 with 24,899 tractors made, accounting for 26 percent of IH's tractor production. The company's share of the U.S. market reached 55 percent that year, and the Farmall's share of that larger market was 14.5 percent. The Fordson's share of the market had remained high as Ford sold tractors below cost at $395 and then $420 after October 1, 1923. But faced with a shrinking market, 1928 was the last year the Fordson was made in the United States. Ford then moved Fordson production to Cork, Ireland, and later to Dagenham, England. Fordson tractors were imported into North America but never in the staggering numbers of the days of U.S. production in the early 1920s.

Farmall production peaked in 1930 with 42,093 tractors produced. In that same year, total Farmall production passed 100,000 tractors at the Farmall Works in Rock Island, Illinois. Total production through 1932 was 134,647 Farmalls, with the model now referred to as the Regular. IH's P. Y. Timmons of the Farm Sales Department observed in 1932 that at least nine out of ten all-purpose tractors in the field that year were Farmalls. The all-purpose machine was indeed fulfilling Bert Benjamin's hopes and dreams.

Not only did the Farmall expand the way farmers used a tractor on the farm, it spawned multiple Farmall models and a deluge of row-crop imitators across the industry. As historian Wayne G. Broehl observed in his comprehensive book on the agricultural implement industry, *John Deere's Company: A History of Deere & Company and its Times*, "It is difficult to overemphasize the breakthrough in farming technology brought by this one new tractor. The response from the field was instantaneous—the Farmall became an abiding success."

1928 Farmall from behind

Above: *The wide Farmall drawbar provided choices for hitching drawn equipment. With the drawbar removed and the cultivator attached, the Farmall's wide rear stance permitted it to straddle two 40- to 42-inch (100- to 105-cm) corn rows while its tricycle front ran down the middle of the rows. High clearance beneath the rear axles allowed it to cultivate corn as tall as two feet (60 cm) without breaking the stalks.*

1928 Farmall

Right: *Restored to like-new condition by collector Robert Lessen of Hartsburg, Illinois, this 1928 Farmall shows the features that finally won the 1920s Tractor War and sent the Fordson off to Ireland and England in search of greener pastures. The Farmall was an honest two-plow tractor for primary tillage, drove belt-operated equipment with its belt pulley, powered drawn harvesting equipment with its PTO, mounted a mower on the rear for mowing, accurately cultivated row crops with its front-mounted cultivator, and was easy to drive and operate—and all of that from one machine. The Farmall was engineered to turn in its own length so it could exit one pair of rows and pivot around into the next row pair. Cables connected by a lever on the front steering spindle actuated rear wheel brakes when the steering wheel was cranked to its extreme turn position. The Farmall started on gasoline and burned kerosene or distillate. In 1928, nearly 25,000 Farmalls were built at the Rock Island Farmall Works at Rock Island, Illinois.*

Father of the Farmall

Farm boy Bert R. Benjamin, a native son of Jasper County, Iowa, is credited by many as being the "Father of the Farmall." Although IH generally shared the Farmall's creation with its team of engineers, it was obviously Benjamin's staunch belief in and defense of the "Farm-All" concept that kept it alive and pushed it to a successful completion against staggering odds, including opposition within IH.

Benjamin was born December 17, 1870, on a farm near Newton, Iowa. From a modest rural start, he grew into one of the key players in the development of International's revolutionary Farmall tractor, a machine that pushed human farm productivity and efficiency to new heights, and created an entirely new type of farm tractor.

Benjamin was the son of Jonathan and Louisa Boydson Benjamin, a pioneer Jasper County farm family. Young Bert attended local schools, worked on the family farm, taught in a local elementary school, and in 1893, graduated with a degree in agricultural engineering from Iowa Agricultural College in Ames, now Iowa State University. He soon went to work as a helper in the Experimental Department at McCormick Harvesting Company in Chicago. He worked for a time as a draftsman in the Experimental Department. By 1901, he was named chief inspector there, a position he held when International Harvester was formed in 1902. He held the chief inspector post until 1910 when he became superintendent of the Experimental Department at McCormick Works.

Benjamin cemented his ties with his home community in 1903 when he married Wilhelminia Bergman, the younger sister of Mrs. F. L. Maytag, whose husband, Fred, founded the famous appliance company that still bears the Maytag name. Thus, Bert Benjamin and Fred Maytag were brothers-in-law.

It was during his time as superintendent of the Experimental Department—about 1911 as he later remembered it—that Benjamin first began to envision a machine that would do more than just pull trailed implements from its drawbar.

In 1919, working on developing new implements aimed at what was then called "power-farming," Benjamin devised a power-driven binder and equipped the company's International 8/16 tractor with a rear power take-off to run the binder. It was an industry first to power implements with power "taken off" the tractor. Before the PTO, drawn implements needing rotary motion relied on power taken off one of the implement wheels by a powertrain of gears and chains, or an auxiliary gasoline engine was installed on the implement to supply the needed power. In wet, muddy conditions, the implement wheel "tapped" to supply implement power would often slide to a stop and leave the implement powerless. Auxiliary power units worked well, but added to the cost of the trailed implements.

The PTO was a factory-offered option on the 15/30 and 10/20 McCormick-Deering tractors sold beginning in 1922. PTOs were soon available on almost all farm tractors and more equipment was developed to use that power, including binders, corn pickers, rear-mounted mowers, and other machines. Benjamin had made the tractor more valuable by making its power available through the PTO to run pulled equipment.

His idea of adding even more utility to tractors to make them into "Farm-All" machines was beginning to take shape as he worked to add implements to the failing IH Motor Cultivator. The clumsy machine served as a valuable test-bed for new ideas in adapting equipment to an all-purpose machine carrying a power source. But the old Motor Cultivator did not do anything well. It was top heavy, too lightweight, underpowered, slow, and hard to steer. However, it held the germ of an idea whose time had come, that of a universal or general-purpose tractor that could handle all farm chores.

One by one its flaws were addressed and remedied, and from those efforts emerged a new type of farm tractor. Tractor-type drive wheels were substituted for the old cultivator wheels, and a chain drive through a high axle gave it crop clearance and more traction. Subsequent experimental versions saw the engine mounted to the frame with its four vertical cylinders aligned with the direction of travel.

But it was not until engineers gave up on making the Farm-All work in two directions that the parts of the tractors started to fall into place. If it traveled forward, like a tricycle, the cultivator could be front-mounted where it could be seen and controlled. By placing the cultivator just rear of the front wheel axle, the cultivator gangs would steer quickly to dodge errant plants, a need in cross-cultivating corn. Coupling the cultivator gangs to the steering made that dodging action immediate for good control at higher, more productive speeds.

The rear axle was left elevated, and gears in a sturdy housing dropped power from the gearbox down to the wheels; the setup gave more crop clearance. Steering of the two front tricycle wheels was augmented with brakes that were self-applied by the steering wheel in short turns. A rear-mounted, centered PTO was made standard to power machines being especially designed for it.

The resulting machine showed enough promise in its early tests to warrant Benjamin's championing of the concept throughout the company. Benjamin faced an uphill battle at IH to move the Farmall into production. That opposition was due partly to a poor farm economy, two other new tractor models being introduced by IH, and a smattering of internal politics. But it's clear his project was developing growing support. In 1922, he was promoted to assistant to the chief engineer at IH, a corporate-level position that must have given him a little more muscle to sell his Farmall concepts.

Years later, Benjamin remembered being pretty much alone in his support for the Farmall. But as he began to gather information from field trials of experimental tractors, his interoffice letters and memos were more specific as to the economic advantages of the Farmall to the farmer. The 1923 field trials of twenty-six of the "new" lightweight Farmall gave him lots of ammunition. The Farmall could, for instance, save $7.30 per acre in costs in growing corn and $10.20 per acre in cotton compared with farming with horses. Those differences, Benjamin pointed out, were extra profit to the farmer. The 1923 experimental Farmalls were a success, and Benjamin began to make converts of company officials one by one to his Farmall cause. Enthusiasm came from the field too. One Texas farmer observed of the experimental Farmall he was using, "It's homely as the devil, but if you don't want to buy one you'd better stay off the seat."

In late 1923, IHC decided to build 200 Farmalls for sale. The first one, serial QC-501, was shipped to Taft, Texas, on February 29, 1924. Benjamin made yearly visits to the farm where QC-501 was operating to keep in touch with his Farmall progeny. He was proud to report back that the first production Farmall planted and cultivated 200 acres (80 hectares) of cotton per year for seven years at a repair cost of about $20 annually, including new pistons and sleeves. With a four-row cultivator available in 1926, the cost of cultivating cotton there dropped to 12 cents per acre with the Farmall, compared with a cost of 50 cents per acre using mules.

Benjamin leaned on his practical personal experience gained on the home farm in Iowa as the basis for the concept and development of the Farmall. That farm experience served him, IH, and the row-crop farmer well. Benjamin received more than 140 different patents in his forty-seven years with IH, many of them key patents on the Farmall and its specially designed implements.

Among the recognition Benjamin received for his work on the Farmall was the 1943 Cyrus Hall McCormick gold medal for outstanding contributions to the farm equipment industry presented by the American Society of Agricultural Engineers. In 1968, his alma mater, Iowa State University College of Engineering, awarded him its Professional Achievement Citation in Engineering. Benjamin also received a gold medallion from the government of France for "service to agriculture."

Bert Benjamin retired from IH in 1939. He died at the age of 99 in October 1969.

Chapter 5

The Farmall Family

The Row-Crop Tractor that does All Farm Jobs
within Its Power Range.
—Deere GPWT ad playing on the
Farmall name, 1930

Above: **Farmall F-12 brochure**

1939 Farmall 20
Left: *Built from 1932 through 1939, the popular F-20 sold 148,690 units.*

The success of the Farmall was so great that International began to build on its all-purpose concept with similar tractors in a range of horsepower sizes. Where there had been but one Farmall Regular, there were soon three different models.

A big three-plow sibling to the original Farmall, the Farmall 30, or F-30, added to the available row-crop power on North American farms beginning late in 1931. The F-30 was a larger-scale version of the familiar Farmall Regular, weighing 5,300 lb (2,385 kg), or about 1,500 pounds (675 kg) more than the original. Its four-cylinder IH engine had 4.25x5.00-inch (106.25x125-mm) bore and stroke and turned at 1,150 rpm, cranking out 20.7 drawbar and 30.29 belt hp. Its four-speed transmission gave it ground speeds of 2, 2⅝, 3¼, and 3⅞ mph (3.2, 4.2, 5.1, and 6.2 km/h) forward and 2½ mph (4 km/h) in reverse. It later had a high-speed transmission when it was delivered on factory-installed pneumatic rubber tires.

The F-30 was in direct horsepower competition with the McCormick-Deering 15/30. By the time of the F-30's introduction in 1931, IH had decided that the potential increased sales of the F-30 as a row-crop machine compared with losing sales of the 15/30 standard tractor might more than balance out. IH had already seen this happen when the original Farmall took away sales from the standard 10/20 but resulted in higher overall sales.

Only 683 F-30s came out of the Farmall Works in 1931. Production jumped to 3,122 tractors in 1932 but slumped to 1,222 tractors as the Great Depression hit bottom in 1933. Gradual improvement in 1934 sales moved production up to a nominal 1,506 tractors, and real progress began to show in 1935 when 3,375 F-30s rolled out the door. Production more than doubled in 1935 to 8,057 tractors and peaked at 8,502

1936 F-30 Farmall

In late 1931, IH introduced the big F-30 Farmall, a scaled-up version of the original Farmall said to be the "big-farm" member of the Farmall family. Its 4.25x5-inch (106.25x125-mm) engine was equipped to burn gasoline, kerosene, or distillate. It produced more than 20 drawbar hp to pull a three-bottom plow in most conditions to turn from 9 to 16 acres (3.6–6.4 hectares) per day. Features and farm utility were much the same as the original Farmall, but on a larger scale. Harold Glaus of Nashville, Tennessee, grew up with this tractor his parents bought used just before he was born.

1936 Farmall F-30

Capable of producing 30 belt hp, the F-30 could handle a 28-inch (70-cm) thresher and the larger sizes of ensilage cutters, husker-shredders, hammer mills, and other belt machines. Its farm work output could replace ten to fourteen horses, according to IH, and use only 25 to 30 gallons (95–114 liters) of fuel per day. With the advent of the F-30 in 1931, the original Farmall was referred to as the Regular.

1936 Farmall F-30
Above, top: *The F-30's crop-clearing height for the rear axles was achieved with gears housed in these enclosures on the rear axles.*

1936 Farmall F-30
Above, bottom: *The F-30 featured enclosed steering gears as compared with the open gears of the original Farmall. Rubber tires soon replaced steel wheels.*

machines in 1937. Combined 1938 and 1939 production added a modest 2,841 more tractors to the total count of 29,526 F-30s produced during its eight-year production run.

Replacement for the Original Farmall

The replacement for the venerable original Farmall Regular came in 1932 with an improved and slightly larger version called the Farmall 20. The F-20 got a power boost of about 10 percent to a Nebraska test rating of 16.12 drawbar and 24.13 belt hp. It was still a two-plow tractor like the Regular, but it now could pull those two bottoms somewhat faster.

The F-20, like the larger F-30, was equipped with a four-speed transmission with 2⅜, 2¾, 3¼, and 3¾ mph (3.8, 4.4, 5.2, and 6 km/h) forward speeds and 2⅞ mph (4.6 km/h) reverse. Its familiar IH engine had a bore and stroke of 3.75x5.00 inches (93.75x125 mm) and was governed at 1,200 rpm under load. Like its predecessor, it could burn gasoline, kerosene, or distillate. IH's FL-4 magneto and a Zenith Model K-5 carburetor came standard.

Wheelbase of the F-20 was 85 inches (212.5 cm). By using dished cast rear wheels, tire tread was adjustable from 68 up to 96 inches (170–240 cm) center to center to fit row widths of 34 and 48 inches (85 and 120 cm). PTO and a belt pulley came as standard equipment on the F-20 as they had on the Regular.

The F-20 became International's most popular Farmall tractor to date with a production run of close to 150,000 tractors from its start in 1932 to 1939 when the F-20 line was closed for a replacement machine. Its sales started well with 2,500 built in 1932. In 1933, it was turned out at a respectable rate of 3,380 tractors. The Great Depression caught up with the F-20 in 1934 when only 662 were built. As the Depression waned in 1935, an amazing 26,334 F-20s rolled off the line. Production peaked in 1936 at 36,033 tractors, and figures were nearly as good in 1937 at 35,676 units. Another good production year was experienced in 1938 with 25,268 tractors. In 1939, as the model F-20 neared replacement, 13,111 tractors were built.

Debut of the Farmall F-12

Yet another Farmall debuted in 1933, ironically just in time for the Depression. The Farmall 12 or F-12 introduced several concepts new to the Farmall line. The F-12 was smaller, and it took a different approach

to crop clearance at the rear axles. Instead of the rear drive axles being geared from the differential down through a "drop box," as on the Regular, the F-30, and the F-20, the single-piece large-diameter axles on the F-12 rear end projected straight out and had large-diameter wheels hub-mounted to them.

Oliver Chilled Plow Company had used straight axles and a "floating" hub on a prototype row-crop tractor designed and patented by Oliver engineer Herman Altgelt some years before Oliver's 1929 merger with Hart-Parr. J. I. Case Threshing Machine Company had used large wheels bolted to fixed hubs on its production 1930 Model CC row-crop tractor.

The design as used on the F-12 eliminated the extra weight of the old Farmall's housing and gears and substituted larger-diameter wheels and a single-piece rear axle to provide the needed crop clearance. Tread adjustment now became as simple as jacking up the tractor, loosening bolts on the wheel hub, sliding the wheels to the desired tread width, then re-tightening the hub bolts.

Night work

Above: *Equipped with rubber tires and a front-mounted four-row planter, this F-30 is extending the working day by planting at night. Rubber tires became a popular option in the mid-1930s. Generators, electric starters, and lights soon followed. Note the long exhaust pipe extension. It helped move the exhaust noise above the operator. (Photo courtesy State Historical Society of Wisconsin #WhiI-767-W 7-10)*

Red F-30

Facing page: *IH changed its tractor color from gray to red on November 1, 1936. This 1937 narrow-tread F-30 sports the new color. Narrow-tread versions helped fit the tractors to closer-spaced row crops. Don Rimathe of Huxley, Iowa, owns this F-30.*

Big Farmalls

Above: *F-30 Farmalls were manufactured from 1931 until 1939 with some inventory sold as late as 1940. Records show 29,526 of the big tractors made. Attachments included a wide front end.*

Left: **1936 Farmall F-20 literature**

The F-12 mounted adjustable rear drive wheels of 54 inches compared with 40- or 42-inch-diameter wheels on the F-20 (135 versus 100 or 105 cm). The concept worked, and when new Farmalls were introduced in 1939, the two larger models adapted it—as did most all competing row-crops built after the F-12's introduction. The F-12 rear tread was adjustable between 44 and 78 inches (110–195 cm) so it could straddle two rows as narrow as 22 inches (55 cm) through two rows as wide as 39 inches or a few inches wider (97.5+ cm).

The F-12's IHC four-cylinder 3.00x4.00-inch (75x100-mm) engine had an operating speed of 1,400 rpm. Nebraska tests showed 12.31 drawbar and 16.2 belt hp from the gasoline-burning version; the kerosene burner tested slightly lower. The F-12 was a small two-plow machine, more at home with two 12-inch (30-cm) bottoms than the two fourteens (35-cm) that many people hitched it to. Pre-production F-12s built in 1932 were equipped with Waukesha engines, as were a few tractors produced in 1933. Later production all used the valve-in-head IH engine. Its three-speed transmission pulled it along at 2¼, 3, and 3⅞ mph (3.6, 4.8, and 6.2 km/h) forward and 2¼ mph (3.6 km/h) in reverse. Later versions on rubber tires got a speed boost.

Farmall Attachments

Implements made by IH to attach directly to the F-12 included a front-mounted two-row cultivator, rear-mounted PTO-driven sickle-bar mower, and rear two-row lister planters for corn, cotton, beans, and other seeds. Quick Attach fastened them quickly and securely to the Farmall's rear axle.

The Depression failed to daunt the little F-12. In fact, its low price of $607.50 and its smaller specifications made it fit the hard times. Its inaugural year of 1933 saw 4,355 tractors built. In 1934, when other tractor sales were tumbling, its sales were stubbornly persistent and production rose to 12,530 units. In 1935, it more than doubled in production to 31,249. Sales held on in 1936 with a modest increase to 33,177 and peaked in 1937 at 35,681 tractors. With its replacement coming on line in 1938, F-12 production dropped to 6,425 tractors. Total F-12 production from 1932 through 1938 amounted to 123,442, including the 25 pre-production F-12s made in 1932.

Arrival of the F-14

The last model in the Farmall F Series was an F-12 look-alike, the F-14, built in modest numbers between 1938 and 1939. About the only visible differences from the F-12 were that the F-14 had its steering column raised by way of a bracket at the rear of the gas tank, and it sported a three-spoked steering wheel of larger diameter than the F-12's cast four-spoked wheel. The driver's seat was raised on the F-14 as well. Rubber-tired F-14s also used a cast rear wheel.

The inside differences consisted of an engine operating speed increase from 1,400 to 1,650 rpm. Its Nebraska tests rated the F-14 at 14.84 drawbar and 17.44 belt hp. Total production in its two-year life was 31,903 tractors with 15,607 made in 1938 and 16,296 in 1939.

Rubber Tires and the Color Red

Two changes in appearance effected the F Series during its production. Only one of those changes boosted the tractor's performance.

Pneumatic rubber tires began to be offered as factory options on International tractors starting in 1933. Although they added to initial tractor cost compared with steel wheels, farmers realized they would soon pay for themselves in increased efficiency and productivity.

University of Illinois trials of rubber-tired tractors versus steel-lug-equipped tractors indicated a 20–25 percent gain in useable drawbar horsepower with the rubber tires. In addition, rubber-tired tractors had a 25 percent saving in fuel for heavy pulling and an average fuel saving of 14–17 percent in year-round use. University of Nebraska test results were similar and compared rubber with steel wheels for cultivating, combining wheat, binding oats, drilling wheat, picking corn, plowing, and moving hay. The rubber-tired operations showed a 13.1 percent saving in time and a 17.9 percent savings in fuel. At an added cost for rubber tires of about $200, Iowa State University researchers determined that a tractor had to be used about 500 hours (or fifty ten-hour days) to recover the extra cost for rubber tires. The result of the research and the farmers' own experiences brought a rapid switch to pneumatic tractor tires. By 1938, most new tractors were being delivered on rubber tires.

Along the learning curve during acceptance of

1939 Farmall F-20

Above: *Piqua, Ohio, IH collector Tom Hill equipped his 1939 F-20 with nearly all of the options available when the tractor was made. The wide front was popular when tractor uses required extra stability. Built from 1932 through 1939, the popular F-20 sold 148,690 units in that period.*

1939 Farmall F-20

Left: *First introduced in 1932, the F-20 replaced the Regular Farmall in the IH row-crop tractor lineup. The F-20 engine was a touch stronger than the old Regular and put out 16 drawbar and 24 belt hp. By the time this F-20 was built in 1939, it could be equipped with a generator, starter, and lights as well as rubber tires.*

rubber tires, it was realized that added weight, especially on lighter tractors like the Farmalls, would minimize slippage or wheel "creep." To start with, concrete wheel weights were devised, but they were soon replaced with cast-iron weights. Then, a non-freezing solution of water and calcium chloride was injected into the inner tubes in the pneumatic tires. A needed air pocket at top of the tube still let the tires "bounce," and the water solution provided weight directly over the tractor's rubber tread.

Rubber-tired tractors soon became almost standard in the industry, except for a period during World War II when defense needs kept rubber off the farm, and steel wheels and lugs briefly returned.

The non-performing change made to International tractors November 1, 1936, had its own popu-

1932 Farmall F-12 pre-production model

Above: *Hailed as the answer to the power problems of the farmer with limited acreage, the F-12 got its trial starting in fall 1932 with twenty-five pre-production models like this one owned by James Gall of Reserve, Kansas. Powered with a Waukesha FL 3x4-inch (75x100-mm) engine that turned at 1,400 rpm, the new little tractor went into regular production in Chicago in 1933. The unusual single wheel was soon replaced with other types, including the two steel wheels often seen on the tractor. Gall bought this F-12, serial number FS 511, from its original owner in Hortonville, Kansas. The pre-production tractors were preceded by five experimental F-12 models shipped for testing in May and June 1932.*

Right: **1936 product literature on Farmall F-12**

Farmall F-12 pre-production model

Above, top: *The pre-production F-12 with the Waukesha engine had the air cleaner mounted on the right side of the radiator grille. About 2,500 early 1933 F-12s used the Waukesha flathead engine until IH replaced it with its own valve-in-head engine. IH used its own magneto on the F-12. Most of the room above the head on the engine was taken up by the valve cover on the later IH engine.*

Farmall F-12 pre-production model

Above, bottom: *Rear differential of the 1932 pre-production F-12.*

lar appeal and was to greatly enhance their overall looks. It was from that date that new IH farm tractors lost their gray color scheme and were painted all red instead. The color specified for tractor paint from that day on was Harvester No. 50 motor truck enamel. Ground-contacting wheels or tracks were to be painted with Harvester red varnish.

Farmall Tractor Family

The three Farmall models soon began to generate new tractor models designed for more specific uses. The Regular set the pattern with its spin-off cousin named the Farmall Fairway. Smooth, wide rims replaced the usual angled lugs permitting the modified Farmall to be used on lawns, turf, or sod without the lugs tearing up the surface. Small spike lugs could be added to the rims when additional traction was needed. The Fairway found a ready market on golf courses, sod farms, and even airports still using grass runways. The introduction of pneumatic tires in the mid-1930s soon eliminated the need for a specialized sod and turf tractor. Serial numbers of Fairway tractors are not differentiated from Farmall production.

W-12, I-12, O-12, and Fairway-12

Standard-tread tractors based on the Farmall F-12 included the compact and "cute" W-12, I-12 industrial, O-12 orchard, and Fairway-12 versions. The Fairway-12 was basically the O-12 but with either wide steel wheels with turf spikes or later, when rubber tires were available, turf tires.

Parts commonality between the 12 Series tractors helped IH keep production costs down. All used the same 3.00x4.00-inch (75x100-mm) bore-and-stroke four-cylinder engine as in the F-12 and showed similar power of about 10 drawbar and 14–16 belt hp. Different rpm settings suited to each tractor's application were used. Frames and front ends were the same in all models, giving the 12 Series a common wheelbase of 60 inches (150 cm) and a turning radius of about 9 feet (2.7 m). Tractor weight was about 2,900 lb (1,305 kg) on the W-12 up to 3,200 lb (1,440 kg) for the O-12 with its extra fenders and shielding.

Starting with production in 1934 and ending in 1938, there were 3,630 W-12 standard tractors made. W-14 production in 1938 and 1939 added another 1,162 tractors for a total of 4,793 of the small W Series. The orchard O-12 tractor and its O-14 sibling

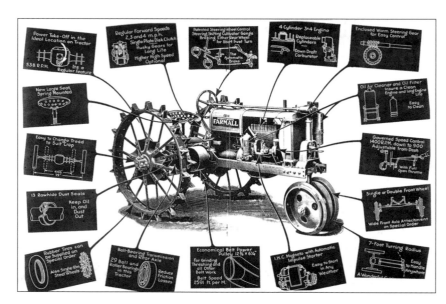

Popular features of the Farmall F-12

Row-crop specialist
Like the other Farmalls, the F-12 was a specialist at cultivating row crops. This F-12 is cultivating potatoes in 36-inch (90-cm) rows with the two-row "armstrong" lift cultivator. At row end, the operator stood on the platform and used the lift levers to raise the cultivator before turning the tractor around into the next pair of rows—note the sweat stains on the driver's jacket. This tractor was in use on 200 acres (80 hectares) of British Queen potatoes near Encinitas, California. (Photo courtesy State Historical Society of Wisconsin #WhiI-483-Y)

sold about 3,776 tractors between 1934 and 1939. Industrial I-12 and I-14 versions totaled 3,087 tractors from 1934 through 1939.

McCormick-Deering W-30

In-house competition impacting both the McCormick-Deering 15/30 and the 10/20 came from the W-30 standard-tread tractor launched in 1932. Based on the F-30's four-cylinder 4.25x5.00-inch (106.25x125-mm) engine, the W-30's integral frame and other construction resembled that of the 15/30 and 10/20, but was a new design. No side engine covers were used on the W-30. A flyball governor helped keep the W-30 engine at its rated 1,150 rpm to produce the 4,820-lb (2,169-kg) tractor's 19.69/31.31 hp. It came with a three-speed transmission producing speeds of 2½, 3¼, and 3¾ mph (4, 5.2, and 6 km/h). Reverse was 2¾ mph (4.4 km/h).

Compared with the spread-out row-crop F-30, the W-30 was a smaller tractor in weight and dimensions. Its wheelbase was just over 6 feet (180 cm) long, its rear tread 53¼ inches (133 cm) wide, and its total width only 66¼ inches (166 cm). It provided a lot of power in a small package and soon became a favorite in orchards and vineyards. Its 1935 price of $975 on steel was $125 less than the 15/30 and only $100 more

1937 Farmall F-12
Steel wheels and lugs were available in a wide range of types for different soil conditions. These spade-type lugs were fitted to a narrow rim and were adjustable as to angle. Collector Jim Gall of Reserve, Kansas, has many of the steel-wheel types used on the F-12 and the Regular Farmall.

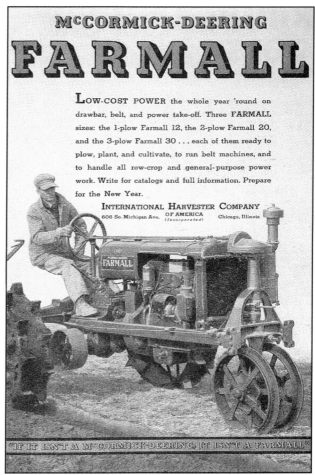

Above: **1934 Farmall advertisement**

1939 Farmall F-14

Left: *The last of the F Series tractors joined the IH line in 1938 with the F-12 look-alike F-14. IH tweaked the engine by increasing its speed to 1,650 rpm for a power output of 14.84 drawbar and 17.44 belt hp. This late-model F-14 has the steel wide-front available as an option. The steering wheel was raised at the rear and the operator's seat was boosted, but outwardly the F-14 looks like its predecessor, the F-12. John Bossler of Highland, Illinois, restored this machine. Made only in 1938 and 1939, just 31,903 F-14s were built.*

than the much smaller 10/20. The W-30 was built from 1932 until 1940 with a total production of 32,531 tractors made. An industrial version, the I-30, was also offered.

McCormick-Deering W-40, WK-40, and WD-40

A standard tractor of larger size and power came with the introduction of the big McCormick-Deering W-40 in 1934. Initially called the WA-40, the model designation became the W-40 once the kerosene- and distillate-burning WK-40 arrived.

For the first time ever on its wheeled tractors, IH used a six-cylinder engine in the 6,633-lb (2,985-kg) W-40. Its closest IH relatives were the firm's track-type tractors rather than the Farmall. The W-40's six-cylinder engine had been used as early as 1932 in the International crawler TracTracTor TA-40.

The gas engine of the W-40 had a 3.625x4.50-inch (90.625x112.5-mm) bore and stroke and turned at 1,600 rpm under load. The kerosene-distillate WK-40 had a slightly larger bore of 3.75 inches (93.75 mm) with the same 4.50-inch (112.5-mm) stroke. The three W-40 models were considered four-plow machines and many also saw heavy use on the belt.

The WD-40 diesel version used the same four-cylinder diesel as the TD-40 diesel TracTracTor, a 4.75x6.50-inch (118.75x162.5-mm) bore and stroke engine that turned over at 1,100 rpm to produce about 30 drawbar and 44 belt hp. It was the first use of a diesel engine in a wheeled tractor in the United States. The IH diesel was started on gasoline and switched over to diesel as it warmed up. The WD-40 was heavier than the gas and kerosene tractors, tipping the scale at 7,550 lb (3,398 kg).

The W-40 Series was made between 1934 and 1940. Production for the three variations totaled just over 10,000 tractors. The diesel WD-40 made up 3,370 units of that total, or more than a third of the W-40 Series production. The I-40 and ID-40 industrial counterparts only sold about 350 tractors.

Hydraulic lift
Above, top: *The hydraulic lift offered for the F-12 in 1936 was powered from the left end of the pulley shaft in the tractor transmission. The lift was mounted to the top of the transmission housing under the tractor seat.*

Power implement lifting and lowering
Above, bottom: *Powered cranks on the transmission-mounted hydraulic lift unit raised and lowered the Farmall F-12's Quick Attach implements without the back-breaking levers once used.*

1935 Farmall F-12

Rex Miller of Savannah, Missouri, restored this 1935 Farmall F-12. In a departure from the other Farmall tractors, IH dispensed with the gearing that gave crop clearance on the F-20 and F-30 tractors, and on the F-12 used sliding wheel hubs on straight axles with larger-diameter wheels to increase under-axle clearance. The hubs slid on the axle to adjust the rear wheels to different row spacings. Fenders were a popular option to help keep the operator out of the steel lugs. The steering wheel has been raised on this tractor, like on the later F-14. Its low price of just over $600 saw the F-12 weather the Depression with decent sales. Total F-12 production until it was replaced in 1939, was 123,442 machines.

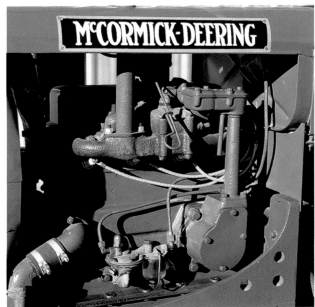

12 Series engine
Above, top: *The same 3x4-inch (75x100-mm) four-cylinder engine appeared in all the 12 Series tractors. They were equipped to burn either gasoline or kerosene-distillate fuels.*

Above, bottom: **1936 W-12 literature**

Small standard tractor
Left: *A total of 3,630 of these little W-12 standard-tread models were made by IH from 1934 to 1938. W-14 production from 1938 and 1939 added another 1,162 units for a total of 4,793 W-12 and W-14 tractors built.*

Golf specialist
International Fairway 12s were a welcome addition to golf course maintenance chores. Wide rims gave them flotation to walk softly over turf.

Kerosene equipment
Kerosene-burning 12 Series tractors were equipped with a heat shroud to raise intake air temperature.

Inset tank
Gasoline for starting the kerosene tractors was held in the small tank inset in the hood. Kerosene F-12s had them too.

Fairway 12 seat
Operators of the little 12 Series rode in this padded seat.

Fairway 12 controls
Above: *Engine controls were next to the steering wheel.*

Fairway 12 spikes
Right: *Small steel spikes on the wide rims aided Fairway traction.*

McCormick-Deering W-30

Above: *Based on the engine from the F-30 Farmall, the small but mighty W-30 came on the scene in 1932 and soon replaced the 15/30, which dated back to 1921. IH dispensed with the side sheets of the earlier model. Power as tested at Nebraska was 19.69 drawbar and 31.31 belt hp, both comparable with the Farmall F-30. Its three-speed transmission was updated to four speeds on the units factory equipped with pneumatic rubber tires. Like the row-crop F-30, the W-30 was a full three-plow tractor. When production ended in 1940, 32,531 W-30s had been made.* (Photo courtesy State Historical Society of Wisconsin #WhiI-1190-W 12-8)

Left: **1936 O-12 literature**

W-40 pulley
Above: *The W-40's pulley transmitted up to 40 hp to belt-driven machines.*

McCormick-Deering W-40
Left: *Debuting in 1934, the W-40 brought six-cylinder, and then diesel, power to IH farm tractors. This 1939 gas W-40 was restored by Powell Smith of Shelbyville, Tennessee. The W-40 tractors were four-plow machines boasting 30 drawbar and more than 40 belt hp. Kerosene WK-40 and gasoline versions used a six-cylinder engine. The WD-40 got is power from a four-cylinder IH diesel that started on gasoline. The W-40 series was more closely related to the IH TracTracTor crawlers than to the Farmall line. Just over 10,000 W-40 series tractors were made from 1934 to 1940. About a third were diesels.*

Chapter 6

"Crawling" TracTracTors

Sure Footed Power.
—TracTracTor ad, 1950s

Above: **T-4, T-5, and TD-5 brochure**

McCormick-Deering T-20 TracTracTor
Left: *Ground-gripping power of the T-20 TracTracTor was appreciated by western farmers to handle heavy combines on soft ground or hills. This T-20 is helping get the crop out by pulling a McCormick-Deering 41-T combine harvesting standing grain near North Battleford, Saskatchewan. The T-20 was preceded by the first IH crawler, the 10/20 or No. 20.* (Photo courtesy State Historical Society of Wisconsin #WhiI-415-AA 2-10)

Track-type tractors, or crawlers, were achieving increasing popularity in the mid- to late-1920s as a way to maximize overall pulling capacity and reduce slippage from tractors that had shed tons of weight with lighter four-cylinder automotive-type engines. There were growing markets for smaller track-type tractors in specific applications both inside and outside of agriculture where superior flotation on soft ground or ground-grabbing traction was needed. The track tractors were ideal under those tough conditions.

IH experimented with putting tracks on its 1918 International 8/16, its first tractor equipped with a truck-type, vertical inline four-cylinder engine. That work was just experimental but would bear fruit a decade later as the McCormick-Deering 10/20 and 15/30 chassis were adapted to tracks.

Birth of the TracTracTor

By late 1928, the new track-type tractor was dubbed the TracTracTor. Its rear driving sprocket was larger than the front track idler giving the appearance that the tractor was traveling downhill. Production of the little TracTracTor 10/20, or No. 20, amounted to about 1,500 machines between 1928 and 1931. Steering clutches for each track were contained in circular, dome-shaped housings projecting upward from the transmission housing in front of the driver. Levers projecting backward and upward from the housings released the clutch to slow or stop either track for steering the tractor.

When the No. 20 was replaced with the TracTracTor T-20 in 1931, steering clutches had been moved inside the rear of the tractor where they were better contained and each could be removed as a unit for repair. Steering-clutch levers located directly in front of the operator actuated the clutches. Left and right foot brakes helped slow or stop the inside track to tighten turns. T-20s had track-driving rear sprockets and front track idlers of equal diameter.

T-20 power came from the Farmall F-20's 3.75x5.00-inch (93.75x125-mm) four-cylinder engine speeded up from 1,200 to 1,250 rpm. It could run on gasoline, distillate, or kerosene. Shipping weight of the tractor was 6,725 lb (3,026 kg) compared with 3,950 lb (1,778 kg) for the similarly powered row-crop F-20. The extra weight of the crawler tractor helped give the tracks more traction for more pulling power at slower speeds. Power of the T-20 was rated

Illust. 50. McCormick-Deering T-40 TracTracTor.

McCormick-Deering TracTracTors—Models T-20, T-35, TD-35 (Diesel), T-40, and TD-40 (Diesel)—were designed to meet the tractor power needs of farmers and fruit growers in sections where special conditions of soil or field make the crawler type desirable.

These five TracTracTor models have met the most exacting demands of users. One much appreciated feature is the easy accessibility of steering clutches and steering brakes, which can be inspected, adjusted, or quickly removed without disturbing adjacent units.

TracTracTor maneuverability is proverbial. These tractors can be turned in their own length and easily guided in close quarters. The T-20, equipped with orchard features, is a favorite among fruit growers.

There are many other practical TracTracTor features which it will pay any prospective buyer to investigate.

Illust. 51. The TD-40 delivers the power required on the Northwest hillsides.

TracTracTor literature

McCORMICK-DEERING TD-40 TRACTRACTOR—
Economical Diesel Power with Simple Crank Starting

ANY man considering a crawler tractor in the 40-horse-power class will do well to study the adaptability of the TD-40 Diesel TracTracTor to his requirements. Operating with high efficiency on the cheaper grades of fuel, this powerful Diesel-engined crawler is effecting substantial savings for owners in a variety of agricultural activities. More and more large-scale farm operators are finding it not only practical but profitable to "go Diesel."

There are other angles of Diesel economy and efficiency to consider. The Diesel not only uses cheaper fuel but uses less fuel than a conventional engine of corresponding size. Consequently, fuel transportation costs are less. A further point is much in evidence in high-altitude regions where the reduced oxygen supply notably decreases the power output of internal-combustion engines. Because of its relatively greater fuel-burning efficiency the Diesel type of engine holds this power loss to a minimum. Moreover, because of its system of metered fuel injection and its slightly slower and more thorough combustion the Diesel's "lugging" ability is more pronounced than that of conventional engines.

Uniform power combined with the five-speed transmission gives to TD-40 TracTracTor performance remarkable flexibility. Five different engine speeds,

hand-throttled, for each gear shift actually gives the TD-40 twenty-five forward traveling speeds! Add to this the TD-40's simplified starting system (it is cranked by hand as easily as a gasoline engine), improved force-feed lubrication, and easy accessibility for inspection or repairs, and you have a few of the reasons for its rapidly growing popularity in large-scale farming operations. The post card on page 31 will bring full particulars.

WHAT THE TD-40 WILL DO:
☞ 1. In extended farm operations it will do the work cheaper than a conventional tractor of corresponding size. ☞ 2. Will do as much field work in a day as 16 to 30 horses or mules from 15 to 25 gallons of low-priced fuel. ☞ 3. Will meet all major power requirements on farms or ranches of from 300 to 500 acres. ☞ 4. Will plow from 20 to 30 acres a day; double-disk upwards of 40 acres; harrow (depending on equipment) from 60 to 125 acres or more; pull the largest harvester-threshers; and operate other drawbar, belt, and power take-off machines in proportion.

1936 TD-40 literature

T-20 TracTracTor

Above: *Although more expensive than wheeled tractors, the small TracTracTor filled the bill when soil conditions called for it. The T-20 weighed 6,725 pounds (3,026 kg) and could pull more than 18 hp at the drawbar and put out more than 25 belt hp. Its power came from the four-cylinder engine common to the Farmall F-20. It was governed to run at 1,250 rpm, or 50 rpm faster in the T-20. From 1931 to 1940, more than 15,000 T-20s were made. They could burn gasoline or kerosene. (Photo courtesy State Historical Society of Wisconsin #WhiI-657-X 5-2)*

T-40 and TD-40 TracTracTors

Left: *IH took its crawler machines to a larger size level with the T-40 Series beginning in 1932. The gasoline and kerosene T-40s were driven with the IH six-cylinder engines also used in the wheeled W-40s. The diesel versions used the company's four-cylinder diesel engine also found in the WD-40 wheeled tractor. The T-40s weighed 11,705 pounds (5,267 kg) and the TD-40s 12,218 pounds (5,498 kg), or nearly twice the T-20's weight. Four-bottom plows were no problem for the T-40 Series. Of the 7,600 T-40s made from 1932 to 1939, more than two thirds were diesels. (Photo courtesy State Historical Society of Wisconsin #WhiI-438-V)*

1937 T-35 TracTracTor

Improved track design and the use of heat-treated components in the T-35 helped lengthen its track life. It weighed about 1,000 pounds (450 kg) less than the T-40 at 10,800 pounds (4,860 kg) and was slightly less powerful using engines with a smaller cylinder bore. Industrial uses for crawler tractors was growing as IH badged this new tractor as an International, as it customarily did for industrial machines. Production of the T-35 and TD-35 reached 5,587 from 1937 to 1939. Styled TracTracTors with new model designations were on the way. (Photo courtesy State Historical Society of Wisconsin #WhiI-83-AA 1-13)

at 18.33/25.31 hp. By locking one track, the T-20 would spin around in a 12-foot (3.6-meter) circle. Its three-speed transmission produced ground speeds of 1½, 2¾, and 3⅞ mph (2.4, 4.4, and 6.2 km/h) with a 2-mph (3.2-km/h) reverse.

Just over 15,000 T-20s were built from 1931 to 1939. In 1935, the T-20 had a base price of $1,495 when equipped with the 41.5-inch-spaced (103.75-cm) tracks. With the wide tread of 50.5 inches (126.25 cm), the list price was $1,565.

Track covers and an under-mounted air cleaner and exhaust converted the low-profile T-20 into an orchard tractor. Its low center of gravity made it useful on slopes and sidehills where a wheeled tractor might roll over. Its industrial applications helped the

company enter that new and growing market. Small hydraulically operated bulldozer blades were available for the T-20 from several manufacturers.

A TracTracTor based on the McCormick-Deering 15/30, called the Model 15, was apparently limited to only about fifty units made in 1931. A companion for the T-20, a better and bigger crawler was already in the pipeline—the four-plow T-40.

Launch of the T-40 Series

Six-cylinder engines with bore and stroke of 3.625x4.50 inches (90.625x112.5 mm) were used in the larger T-40 Series of track-type tractors IH began building in 1932. It was the same engine as used in the W-40 wheel tractor. The TA-40 was the gasoline

Big International TD-18
New styling graced the TD-18 crawler when it was introduced in late 1938. Full production began in 1939. The big tractor weighed about 11 tons (9,900 kg) and got its 71 drawbar hp from a six-cylinder 691-ci (11,319-cc) diesel. Farm uses were usually limited to extensive operations. When TD-18 production ended in 1949, about 22,000 had been made. Its successor, the TD-18A, was produced until 1955 with more than 11,000 made. (Photo courtesy State Historical Society of Wisconsin #WhiI-1781-LL)

TracTracTor version. The TK-40 kerosene and distillate version had a slightly larger bore at 3.75 inches (93.75 mm). Those engines operated at 1,100–1,600 rpm. The TD-40 used the IH four-cylinder 4.75x6.50-inch (118.75x162.5-mm) diesel engine that turned over from 800 to 1,100 rpm. The TD-40's engine started on gasoline and switched over to diesel as it warmed up. Its diesel engine was also used on the WD-40 wheel tractor, the first U.S. diesel-powered wheel-type tractor.

The TA-40 and TK-40 TracTracTors were rated at 33 drawbar and 43 belt hp, and weighed 11,705 lb (5,267 kg). The TD-40 turned out similar horsepower ratings yet was somewhat heavier at 12,218 lb (5,498 kg). They could all turn around in a 14-foot (4.2-meter) circle. The T-40 crawlers had five-speed transmissions giving them ground speeds of 1¾, 2¼, 2¾, 3⅛, and 4 mph (2.8, 3.6, 4.4, 5, 6.4 km/h). Reverse was 2¼ mph (3.6 km/h).

IH produced more than 7,600 of the three tractors in the T-40 Series from 1932 through 1939. Of these, 5,965 were the diesel-engined TD-40, and the balance were the gas TA-40 and the kerosene-distillate TK-40.

In 1936, the T-40 sold for $2,700 in the standard track width and $2,850 in the wide-track rendition. The standard diesel TD-40 had a list price of $3,450 and the wide-tread was $3,600. Enclosed cabs were available for $70. A popular bulldozer blade for the T-40 Series was made by Bucyrus-Erie. Controlled hydraulically, the blade made a respectable bulldozer out of the T-40s.

Debut of the T-35 Series

With some 7 hp less than the T-40, the T-35 was introduced in 1937. It too was available in gas, kerosene-distillate, and diesel versions. The TD-35 had a four-cylinder diesel engine with 4.50x6.50-inch (112.5x162.5-mm) bore and stroke, or 0.125-inch (3.125-mm) smaller bore than the TD-40. It listed at $2,725 with a wide-tread version available at $2,800. The wide tread helped give it a wider stance for more stability on slopes. The heavier crawlers were favored for pulling big combines on sloping wheat fields in western parts of North America. The T-35 sold for $415 less than the TD-35 diesel.

T-35s were made from 1937 to 1939 with a total production of more than 5,500 tractors. Shipping weight of the T-35 was 10,800 lb (4,860 kg), or about 1,000 lb (450 kg) less than the T-40.

Stylish Crawlers: TD-18 Series

In keeping with styling changes being made to tractors in the late-1930s, famed New York industrial designer Raymond Loewy restyled the new IH tractor line introduced in 1939, and the crawler tractors got his treatment too.

The big, new International TD-18 crawler was the first IH introduced with the Loewy design. It was first seen in 1938 with the now-familiar rounded, pressed sheet-metal grill with its four groups of narrow horizontal slots. Where possible, Loewy considered the operator in designing the machine and raised exhaust stacks above the operator's head, rearranged controls to be more user-friendly, and raised the seat level to give operators a better view of their work.

Pioneering work on the large TD-18 apparently started at IH about 1934 with a series of tractors that

Farm-sized International TD-6
Comparable in power to the M Farmall and the W-6 International, the T-6 and TD-6 both arrived in 1939. They were made until 1956 with 38,449 tractors counted. This TD-6 is shown moldboard-plowing corn stalks. The tractor weighed more than 7,000 pounds (3,150 kg) and produced up to 25 drawbar hp. They could easily pull three- and four-bottom plows. (Photo courtesy State Historical Society of Wisconsin #WhiI-2293-LL)

CHOOSE FROM 3 POWER SIZES
CHOOSE DIESEL OR GASOLINE
CHOOSE THE OPTIONS
YOU NEED

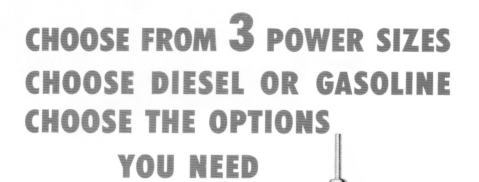

New power and traction for plowing and tillage.

New low-profile power and pull for fruit-farming.

Gasoline

NEW POWER

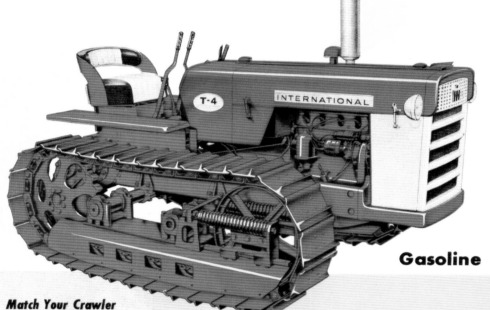

Match Your Crawler To Your Jobs

Standard Transmission (Live) Power Take-Off

Constant-running Power Take-Off

Three-point hitch or swinging drawbar

4 or 5-roller track frame

Torque Amplifier

10-, 12- or 14-inch track shoes

38*, 48 or 68-inch track gauge

With 10" shoes only.

INTERNATIONAL T-4

26.3 Drawbar Horsepower*

Powered by the International C-123 gasoline engine you have 5 forward speed . . . 10 with Torque Amplifier . . . from 1.00 to 6.54 m.p.h. to handle with ease all the jobs in its power range.

Swinging drawbar is standard equipment with 3-point hitch available as an attachment. This latter will operate with all category 1 implements.
Estimated

There's a model specialized to your farm in this new compact IH Crawler trio.

New, flotation—regardless of soft ground conditions.

New push-and-pull power to move earth—dig ponds and trench silos.

4

T-4 literature

NOTHING SPARED TO MATCH POWER TO YOUR JOBS!

INTERNATIONAL T-5

30.9 Drawbar Horsepower*

For the farmer who wants additional gasoline power the new International T-5 is built specially to meet his compact crawler requirements. All the outstanding IH features, torque amplifier, choice of track width, 6-volt starting and electrical system, standard swinging drawbar, 3-point hitch are available, and many others make the T-5 a top work producer.

Gasoline

ON TRACKS FOR YOUR FARM

INTERNATIONAL TD-5

There's top diesel economy plus tough lugging power in this new International TD-5. It is equipped with a more powerful version of the famous International engine that set a new standard of high efficiency in the B-275 tractor. This new crawler is a sure footed, power loaded tractor with speeds from 1 to 6.54 m.p.h. so you can select just the right speed for all jobs. Starts easily in any weather with its 12 volt electrical system.

*Estimated

28.5 Diesel Drawbar Horsepower*

5

T-5 and TD-5 literature

105

remained experimental only. The experimental T-80 had the same steering clutch arrangement as the production T-20 and T-40 TracTracTors. Then the T-60 and TD-65 Series were developed in 1935 and 1936 with an improved placement of the steering clutches. With further improvements in 1937 and 1938 and with Loewy styling added, it was designated the TD-65. No production records for the TD-65 are known, so it too is considered an experimental version.

A highly airbrushed photo of the TD-65 in the IH archives gives the crawler the appearance of being a much larger tractor than the TD-18, perhaps of a horsepower size that IH passed by in favor of smaller or larger crawlers.

The new TD-18 was no slouch when it came to power and weight. It tipped the scales at about 11 tons (9,900 kg) and packed a 691-ci (11,319-cc) diesel engine that was rated at 71 drawbar and 85 belt hp. Bosch fuel injection was featured on the six-cylinder 4.75x6.50-inch (118.75x162.5-mm) diesel engine. Tracks that measured more than 7 feet (2.1 meters) long and 18 inches (45 cm) wide gave it a "foot print" of more than 20 square feet (1.8 square meters). A six-speed transmission let it crawl across the ground at 1½, 2, 2½, 3¼, 4½, and 5¾ mph (2.4, 3.2, 4, 5.2, 7.2, and 9.2 km/h).

Obviously aimed at the construction industry, the big TD-18 went into production in 1939 with more than 600 built that year. It was made until 1949 when it was replaced with the TD-18A, which was built until 1955. About 22,000 TD-18s were made and more than 11,000 TD-18As. Later production versions were able to produce more than 100 hp on the belt. Its farm utility was limited to uses on extensive acreages, heavy-pull subsoiling, land clearing, and land leveling for irrigation.

A sequel to the big TD-18 was the improved TD-20, arriving in 1958 and produced through 1973. Production figures show nearly 26,000 of the tractors were built, including 2,500 of a numbered series of Model 200s in 1958 through 1963, and 470 units made of a Model 201 series from 1961 through 1962. Most of the TD-20s were built during the ten-year period from 1963 to 1973.

Smaller Crawlers: T-6 and T-9 Series
More closely related to the IH farm-sized wheel tractors were the T-6, TD-6, and larger T-9 and TD-9

crawlers introduced in the class of 1939 models.

Nebraska tests in 1940 showed 25 drawbar and 33 belt hp for the gasoline-burning T-6 tractor. The distillate-burning tractor showed slightly less power with 24 drawbar and 31 belt hp. The TD-6 rated 22 drawbar and 31 belt hp. Their engines were the four-cylinder 3.875x5.25-inch (96.875x131.25-mm) engines common to the Farmall M and W-6 wheel tractors. Five-speed transmissions were used in the 7,000-lb (3,150-kg) 6 Series crawlers, and its maximum drawbar pulls of 7,652 lb (3,443 kg) under test came at its lower gear speeds.

The T-6 and TD-6 were built between 1940 and 1956, with a total of 38,449 made. A slightly more powerful 61 Series of the T-6 and TD-6 was manufactured between 1956 and 1959, adding another 2,500 tractors. A further-improved 62 Series made from 1959 to 1969 added 3,920 more T-6s and TD-6s for a combined thirty-year total of about 44,970 T-6 tractors.

Nearly twice as popular was the larger T-9 and TD-9 tractors. The tractors could easily handle five-bottom plows. They shared the C-335 IH four-cylinder engines with the standard McCormick-Deering W-9, WD-9, WDR-9, and International 9 Series industrial tractors. The TD-9 diesel used a four-cylinder 4.40x5.50-inch (110x137.5-mm) engine of 334.5 ci (5,479 cc) and in a 1951 Nebraska test racked up 39.50 drawbar and 46.69 belt hp. That compares with the gasoline T-9's 1941 test of 40.59 drawbar and 46.46 belt hp. The T-9 and TD-9 weighed 5½ tons (4,950 kg) and were built on a heavy cast-iron mainframe designed to have the rigidity to handle the drive components of the larger machine.

Heavy-duty implements including subsoilers, ditchers, and field cultivators could be mounted on the McCormick combination carrier-tool bar. Fingertip hydraulic control made it easy for the operator to control tool depth and to raise the implement for turning at the end of the field. The carrier-tool bar was available for the 6 and 9 Series crawler tractors.

By the time production of the T-9 and TD-9 ended in 1956, an estimated 70,720 had been made. Improved Series 91 and 92 versions built from 1956 to 1974 added another 12,999 machines, and 10,030 Series B/150s made from 1962 to 1974 swelled total T-9 crawler production to more than 93,000 tractors during the thirty-five years it was made.

TD-9 with squadron disk hitch
More popular than the smaller TD-6 crawler, the TD-9 was made in numbers reaching 58,182 tractors between 1939 and 1956. Original gas versions tested 40 drawbar hp, and diesel versions produced only slightly lower numbers from their four-cylinder gas or diesel engines. Double tandem disks made short work of seedbed preparation. Note the optional steel radiator shield. (Photo courtesy State Historical Society of Wisconsin #WhiI-2941-MM)

Larger TD-14 and TD-15

Bigger than the T-9 but smaller than the TD-18 was the all-diesel TD-14, also introduced in 1939. The TD-14 weighed 9 tons (8,100 kg) and pulled 52 drawbar and 62 belt hp when originally tested at Nebraska in 1940. Power came from a four-cylinder 461-ci (7,552-cc) engine driving the crawler through a six-speed transmission. Two reverse speeds allowed the operator to back up at a rapid speed, which was especially handy for bulldozing.

The TD-14 was often equipped with a hydraulically controlled dozer blade and found more construction and industrial applications than farm uses. But with squadron hitches it could work a wide swath in the West where there was plenty of room to turn it around.

From 1939 to 1949, 26,260 copies of the TD-14 were built. An improved TD-14A was made from 1949 to 1955 with 12,540 produced. A numbered version, the Model 141 was built between 1955 and 1956 with about 2,250 made. Between 1956 and 1958, a Model 142 was built in about 4,000 units. It featured an increase in engine rpm that allowed it to show 61 drawbar and 83 belt hp in 1956 Nebraska tests.

The TD-14's replacement was the larger TD-15 manufactured from 1958 to 1973. The TD-15 had a new six-cylinder 4.625x5.50-inch (115.625x137.5-mm) 554-ci (9,075-cc) diesel engine. The new crawler weighed in at 24,555 lb (11,050 kg), or more than 12 tons. Nebraska tests in 1960 showed 77 drawbar hp from the TD-15, 6 hp more than the 71 drawbar hp of the TD-18 in its 1940 test. The TD-15 was tested at a maximum drawbar pull of 21,275 lb (9,574 kg) at a 1.87 mph speed (3 km/h). Total TD-15 production, including numbered 150 and 151 Series, reached 25,330 tractors by 1973.

Cat Catcher

With an avowed goal of not only catching up with Caterpillar, but of passing the world leader in construction equipment, IH undertook an energetic program of development and expansion of its construction equipment after World War II. Among its products was a huge, new track-type tractor that was bigger and more powerful than Caterpillar's legendary D-8.

IH announced its new TD-24 in 1947 with much fanfare as the most powerful tractor in the industry. Nebraska tests in 1950 rated it at 161 drawbar hp—and the TD-24 was too large to test on the dynamometer for belt horsepower. It handily beat the Caterpillar D-8's drawbar pull of 110.6 maximum drawbar hp and also beat out another D-8 challenger, the Allis-Chalmers HD-19 crawler, which tested at 118 maximum drawbar hp.

As tested, the six-cylinder TD-24 weighed more than 42,000 lb (18,900 kg), or 21 tons. Its advertised weight was 37,000 lb (16,650 kg), or somewhat more than 18 tons. Power came from its huge 1,090.6-ci (17,864-cc) six-cylinder diesel engine with 5.75x7.00-inch (143.75x175-mm) bore and stroke. IH installed a then-unusual 24-volt electrical system on its biggest tractor to help it start on gasoline and then convert to diesel.

"Planet Power Steering" was featured on the big crawler, harnessing each track to the final drive through two-speed planetary drives. Hydraulically operated with the steering-clutch handles, the two-speed allowed average-speed turns to be made by gearing down one track through its planetary drive. The advantage was that both the inside and outside tracks were continuously powered during average turns. Steeper turns were effected by completely clutching out the power to one of the tracks, as on most crawler tractors.

During its production run from 1947 to 1959, the TD-24 was tweaked to produce more and more horsepower. The 1954–1956 versions were capable of 155 continuous drawbar hp; from 1957 on, the TD-24 could make 163 hp at its pulling end. Total TD-24 unit production from 1947 until 1959 was about 11,100 tractors. Its 1959 replacement, the TD-25, was made until 1973 in numbers nearing 6,200 tractors.

T-24 Tragedy?

In her book on the demise of IHC, *A Corporate Tragedy: The Agony of International Harvester Company,* author Barbara Marsh blames weaknesses in the T-24 as the start of problems that thwarted IH efforts to take its desired lead in construction equipment. The TD-24 soon developed transmission problems that were costly to fix and gave the machine a black eye. In 1954, Caterpillar produced a big brother to the D-8, the D-9. IH responded to the bigger Cat in 1962 with an even larger crawler, the TD-30, the largest IH crawler ever. It promised 320 hp through a gear drive or a power-shift transmission. Major problems with the transmission led IH to cancel the big tractor after five years and only 690 of them were made.

Larger T-340 Series, Smaller T-4 and T-5 Series

The proliferation of large wheel-type farm tractors in the 1960s pinched down on the market for farm-size crawlers. In 1959, IH introduced the T-340 and TD-340 four-plow crawlers. The TD-340 weighed about 6,695 pounds (3,013 kg) and produced maximum drawbar hp of 32.83. The gas T-340 was comparable in power. They shared the engines powering the International 340 tractor series. They could be ordered with IH Torque Amplifier or a Fast Reverser for bulldozer applications. The T-340 and TD-340 production reached more than 8,000 units between 1959 and 1965.

The T-4, T-5, and TD-5 were smaller track-type machines IH also introduced in 1959. The 21-hp T-4 used a 123-ci (2,015-cc) engine derived from the Super A series of wheel tractor. The T-5 was equipped with a 135-ci (2,211-cc) engine and was rated at 29 drawbar hp. The TD-5 had a 144-ci (2,359-cc) diesel engine and 30 hp. All three tractors were equipped with Torque Amplifier to give them ten effective speeds from their five-speed transmissions. They were made through 1960.

"Plowshares are Swords": IH's World War II Production

Just as International Harvester's new line of styled farm tractors brought out in 1939 was becoming popular, the United States became involved in World War II, and the country shifted to a defense mentality. Like all farm equipment makers in the United States, considerable limitations were placed on IH manufacturing of farm machines because of the need for metals and other raw materials to make armaments. IH soon shifted its emphasis to making war materiel.

IH made 6x6 trucks, ambulances, half tracks, mounts for 57mm anti-tank guns, light tanks, gun carriages, gun tractors, torpedoes, crawler tractors, M-1 Garrand rifles, C-46 aircraft components, and many other defense-related products during the war. Because of its role as a major maker of machines that were used to grow food, IH was able to produce a respectable level of some of its farm machines, and only in 1943 did that production decline.

IH President Fowler McCormick noted in an industry magazine advertisement in 1941, "In America, the greatest food-producing country in the world, it is well to consider that Plowshares are Swords!"

"Tractorettes" training program was instituted to help women tractor operators better understand working with the machines. On the farm, the farm wife, sons, and daughters were also filling in on vacant tractor seats.

In 1944, when war production peaked, IH's sales soared past $500 million for the first time, to $640.5 million. After the war ended in 1945, IH was financially able to confront the postwar period of expansion. As Barbara Marsh, author of *A Corporate Tragedy: The Agony of International Harvester Company*, notes, "It was World War II, not the New Deal, which enabled American industry in general and Harvester in particular to shake off the effects of the Depression."

"Plowshares <u>are</u> Swords"

Chapter 7

Facelift for the Farmalls

There's a proud record of progress between the old "Original" of 1923 and the streamlined red Farmalls of today, with endless improvements in power and machines. A new generation has grown up since that date to hail the Farmall System of Farming.
—"The Farmall System of Farming" brochure, 1940s

Above: **1948 Farmall C**

1940 Farmall M with IH Till Planter
Left: *Purdue University agricultural engineers restored this Farmall M shown equipped with a 1954 IH M-21 Till Planter. The Farmall M gained fame as it soldiered away in farm fields for fifteen years.*

The Farmall family of row-crop tractors took on a modern look in 1939 as a newly designed series of tractor models replaced the square-cornered and angular look of the F-30, F-20, and F-14 tractors. Industrial design was finding its way into agricultural equipment as the Great Depression of the 1930s waned and tractor appearance as well as performance added to marketability.

Sharp corners and square fronts were smoothed and rounded on the new Farmall line starting in the late 1930s. Famed industrial designer Raymond Loewy of New York started off with a redesign of the IH company trademark and logo. Loewy remembered that small beginning in his 1979 book *Industrial Design*. "In view of the power and prestige of International Harvester, I thought their trademark was frail and amateurish. The firm's executives asked me to show them what I had in mind. I left Chicago for New York on the train and sketched a design on the dining-car menu, and before we passed through Fort Wayne [Indiana], International Harvester had a new trademark. It was reminiscent of the front end of a tractor and its operator."

Loewy's firm then moved forward with IH engineers to improve the looks and operation of the IH tractors. Loewy's designs were aimed at making the operator a more important part of the machine by considering the operator's needs when designing the control layout. The big, new 80-hp TD-18 crawler introduced in 1938 was the first unit that showed the Loewy design touches. The distinctive rounded radiator grill with its horizontal slits soon dressed up all of the crawler line, including the T-6, TD-6, T-9, TD-9, T-14, and TD-14.

A New Generation of Farmalls

Engineering and design work on a new line of Farmall tractors had been underway at IH since about 1935, as evidenced by photographs found in the IH archives. Beginning with the basic F-20 chassis in 1935, engineers reworked the machine to include the straight single axles of the F-12 into a design called the F-22.

A new, simpler Farmall tractor was emerging. Photographs show that, from that new component combination, engineers and stylists began to work on tractor design, often creating styling details in clay mockups. By fall 1938, "styled" tractors called the 2T and 3F were being considered. While their styling re-

Above: **Original IHC logo**

Facing page: **New IH corporate identity**

sembled what we later know as the Farmall H and M look, the design was still fluid, and at one time obviously included a centered "Cyclops" headlight poking out of a highly sculpted grill. Some of the archival photos show louvered engine side curtains. The photos show that, by January 1939, the M and H design had the rear of the fuel tank finally rounded off, much as we know it today.

The spanking-new line of Farmall tractors wearing the Loewy styling was the big news from IH in 1939 for row-crop farmers. The four new models were the A, B, H, and M Farmalls, four new tractors in three size categories.

Farmall Models A and B

The new, small-engined Farmalls were the A and B, which shared engines but had different row-crop applications. The two new "Culti-Vision" models were designed to fill the bill for smaller all-purpose row-crop tractors and add to the usefulness already shown by the F-12 and F-14 tractors that the Culti-Vision machines were designed to replace.

The Farmall A was a small machine of about one-plow power. The A had wide-set adjustable-tread front wheels designed to straddle one crop row during cultivation. It achieved its needed row-crop clearance through a dropped rear drive reminiscent of the original Farmall. Its engine and drivetrain were offset to the left of the frame, and the operator sat at the right of the engine for a better view of the cultivator;

113

Farmall shape changes

Above: *A new streamlined look for the Farmall was emerging in the F-22 design of July 1937. The interim design used the large rear wheel and sliding hub of the F-12 with new sculpted sheet metal up front. The engine side panels were dropped and the rear fuel tank was rounded in refinements made later. The forward lean to the grille was kept, but vertical elements were added before the design was finalized. (Photo courtesy State Historical Society of Wisconsin #WhiPP 12356)*

1941 Farmall A

Right: *Culti-Vision was featured on the one-plow Farmall A introduced with the other new IH models in 1939. The engine and drivetrain were offset to the left and the driver sat on the right side for a clear view of the one-row cultivator mounted forward under the tractor. This restored beauty in emerging cotton is owned by Alton and Thalua Garner of Levelland, Texas.*

1941 Farmall ad

New IH Farmalls for 1939, the Models M, H, B, and A

this new design was called Culti-Vision. The A's tread could be adjusted between 40 and 68 inches (100–170 cm) for straddling different row widths. Its 3.00x4.00-inch (75x100-mm) engine turned at 1,400 rpm and showed 16.32/18.34 hp in its 1939 Nebraska test on gasoline. Tests on distillate were a couple of horsepower less. The 1940 price of the A was $575, with starter and lights adding another $31.

The AV high-clearance version added another 6 inches (15 cm) of crop clearance by adding length to the front bolsters and equipping the rear with larger wheels and tires.

The B was much like the A except it was a two-row tricycle with a wide rear tread for straddling two rows. The engine and drivetrain were centered on the axles, and only its steering wheel and operator's platform were offset, giving it Culti-Vision too. The B's rear tread width was adjustable from 64 to 92 inches (160–230 cm) to allow it to straddle and cultivate two 34-inch (85-cm) rows or up to two 46-inch (115-cm) rows. The B also used the dropped rear-gear drive of the A. Both A and B models used the same engine and the same size wheels and tires, 8.00x24 inch (200x600 mm) in the rear and 4.00x15 inch (100x375 mm) in front. The B listed for $605 in 1940.

The production of Model As in different versions including AV, an International A, and, later, Super As and Super AVs, totaled more than 237,000 tractors between 1939 and 1954. The B and its BN narrow-tread variant accounted for another 93,000 unit sales during a shorter production period, from 1939 through 1948. The Model B production run was cut short when it was replaced in 1948 with the Model C Farmall, a more versatile row-crop machine.

Farmall Models H and M

The largest new Farmall, the M, was later to achieve fame as one of the all-time classic American farm tractors. But the more popular of the new M and H pair of row-crop tractors was the smaller tractor, the H.

The new M and H were the largest row-crop models in the new streamlined Farmall fleet. The M was a three-plow tractor to take the place of the hardy F-30, and the H a two-plow machine to replace the famous F-20. The new H and M shared the same wheelbase and frame dimensions for implement interchangeability, but other than that they had little in common.

The M and H adopted the axle design first used on the F-12 in 1933 with heavy axles extending directly from the differential case through heavy rear-axle housings. The rear wheels were hub-mounted to the axles for easy and infinite tread adjustability. The larger-diameter wheels mounted on the axles provided the needed row-crop clearance to replace the dropped-gear arrangement pioneered on the original Farmall and used again on the F-30 and F-20.

Rubber tires were standard, but the tractors could be ordered on steel wheels for less money. Many World War II versions of the H and M were delivered on steel wheels when the war tied up the available supply of rubber. The 1940 price for the M was $1,112 on full rubber, $895 on steel. At the same time the H was $962 on full rubber. The diesel MD on full rubber sold for $1,549.50 in 1941.

Both machines had optional electric lights and starters, belt pulley, PTO, and hydraulic Lift-All. Options like starter and lights typically added another $49.50 to the price. The Lift-All hydraulics was a $35

1941 Farmall A
The operator sat to the right above the row on the Farmall A. Crop clearance came from enclosed rear drive gears that raised the rear axle. It featured IH's 3x4-inch (75x100-mm) engine that furnished 16.32 drawbar hp in Nebraska trials.

package.

The gas-fueled M produced 25.83 drawbar and 33.35 belt hp in its Nebraska tests; the M kerosene results were somewhat lower. The M engine measured 3.875x5.25 inches (96.875x131.25 mm) and was designed to operate at 1,450 rpm. A diesel version, the MD was offered beginning in 1941. Like the earlier IH diesel engines, the MD was started on gas and then switched to diesel once it was running.

More than 378,000 M, MV high-clearance, MD, MDV tractors, and Super M Series tractors were manufactured from 1939 to 1954.

The McCormick-Deering standard versions in the M size were the W-6, WD-6, O-6, OS-6, I-6, and ID-6 tractors. During their production run from 1940 through 1954, the standard 6 Series versions of the three-plow M were made in numbers reaching 56,482 tractors.

The two-plow H had the same equipment options as the larger M. Its 3.625x4.25-inch (90.625x106.25-mm) engine ran at up to 1,650 rpm. In Nebraska tests, the gas version of the H showed 19.3 drawbar and 23.72 belt hp; the kerosene version showed a couple of horsepower less. The rear-wheel tread width on

1941 Farmall A
Front and rear wheel weights improved traction on the little A. The two-row Model B Farmall used the same engine as the A, but it was of tricycle design with the engine centered and the driver seated at the right side above the rear axle.

the H was adjustable to any width between 44 and 80 inches (110–200 cm). In total production between 1939 and 1952, the H, HV high-clearance, and Super H versions totaled more that 425,000 units, surpassing M production by nearly 47,000 tractors.

Farmall H counterparts in standard tractors were the McCormick-Deering W-4, OS-4, O-4, and I-4 models. The O-4 had complete shielding of the rear tires and operator platform to protect orchard and grove trees. The OS-4 had the exhaust and air cleaner undermounted to reduce height for orchard work. Most models of the McCormick-Deering standard

tractors were available with many of the Farmall's options. More than 35,800 4 Series standards were made by IH between 1940 and 1954.

Farmall Model C

In 1948, IH replaced its Farmall B Culti-Vision tractor with a new Farmall C with a more conventional row-crop design. Although the C carried the same 3.00x4.00-inch (75x100-mm) engine of its predecessor, the tractor was more similar in design to the larger M and H models.

The offset steering wheel and seat and geared drop

One-trip planting

Above: *Reducing field tillage trips to one pass was the aim of the IH Till Planter of 1954. It was a concept that proved its worth years later as No-Till planting became popular. The three-plow M replaced the old Farmall F-30 in the Farmall model lineup. Nebraska power tests showed 25.83 drawbar hp from its four-cylinder IH engine. More than 378,000 M, MD, MV, MDV, and Super Ms were made from 1939 through 1954.*

Left: **Farmalls for the Midwest, the H, A, and M**

axles of the B were replaced with a centered operator's seat and steering wheel and the same kind of single-piece rear axles first used on the F-12 and later adapted to the H and M. That feature improved the adjustability of the rear-wheel treads as it had on the earlier row-crop tractors. Rear tread was adjustable from 50 inches out to more than 83 inches (125–207.5 cm). The C was equipped with a new Touch-Control hydraulic system with the ability to exert a down pressure as well as just lifting the implement. Two finger-tip control levers were located just in front and to the right of the steering wheel for ease in controlling hydraulically lifted implements.

The engine operating speed on the Model C was stepped up to 1,650 rpm to give the 3,000-lb (1,350-kg) tractor a slight boost in power to about 15 drawbar and 19 belt hp. It could pull two plow bottoms in average soil conditions. The high, rear-mounted seat and the "wasp waist" of the tractor provided excellent operator visibility of both rows for cultivating.

Between the start of Farmall C production in 1948 and the end of Super C production in 1954, there were more than 178,000 of the tractors made. Model C production reached 66,216 by 1951 when the Super C stepped in.

True to the Farmall pattern, an abundance of implements were available especially for use on the C and Super C. Included were row-crop front-mounted cultivators, rear-mounted sickle bar mowers, rear-mounted plows and disc plows, front- and rear-mounted planters and middlebusters, and even a one-row mounted corn picker.

The Littlest Farmall, the Cub

With its marketing eye on the more than 3 million U.S. farms of 40 acres (16 hectares) or less, IH brought out its smallest Farmall, the diminutive Cub, in 1947. It was a tractor with a "friendly" name intended to be easy to afford and easy to keep.

IH thought it could sell up to 50,000 of the Farmall Cub each year and geared up its Louisville, Kentucky, factory to that end. The Cub soon became a favorite of vegetable growers, truck gardens, nurseries, poultry farms, and large estates. IH was somewhat disappointed with its sales to small tobacco farms, one of its original target markets. In the small farm tractor market, the Farmall A and Cub had competition from the Ford-Ferguson 9N, introduced in 1939, and the

later 2N. By 1948, after the split from Harry Ferguson, Ford's red-bellied Model 8N was selling well all over the United States and especially well in the South.

With an offset design and integral construction similar to the A and B, the Cub was expected to provide the same utility as the As and Bs, but on a smaller scale. It had a 60-ci (983-cc) four-cylinder engine with bore and stroke of 2.625x2.75 inches (65.625x68.75 mm). The engine "hummed" along at 1,600 rpm to produce 8.89 drawbar and 9.76 belt hp. It could pull one 12-inch (30-cm) mounted plow or cultivate one crop row which it straddled with its 8.00x24-inch (20x60-cm) rear and 4.00x12-inch (10x30-cm) front wheels. Tire tread width was adjustable between 40 and 56 inches (100–140 cm).

Wheelbase on the Farmall Cub was 69 inches (172.5 cm), and the tractor height was 76 inches (190 cm). The Cub weighed about 1,590 lb (715 kg). Its three-speed transmission provided speeds of 2.16, 3.15, and 6.49 mph (3.5, 5, and 10.4 km/h) with a reverse of 2.41 mph (3.8 km/h).

The Cub was available with a long line of optional equipment to fit it to the job at hand. Options included electric lights and starter, swinging drawbar, PTO or belt pulley, and a muffler. From 1948 on, the IH two-way Touch-Control hydraulic implement control was an option.

More than seventeen implements were designed specifically for the Farmall Cub, giving it great utility on the small farms and estates where it found a home. Included were undermounted one-row cultivators, side-mounted sickle bar mowers, belly-mounted rotary mowers, front-mounted planters, and, of course, the one 12-inch-bottom (30-cm) mounted plow.

Only in its second year of production did the Cub near its hoped-for 50,000-unit annual production mark; this came in 1948 when the Louisville Works built 46,483 Cubs. The production for 1949 was close too, with 41,483 Cubs. Production dropped to nearly half that in 1950 with 21,918. In 1951, 23,001 tractors were made but an erosion of numbers began in 1952 down to 17,829, then to 17,128 in 1953, and a drop of more than 10,000 units in 1954 down to 7,029, and to 7,217 Cubs in 1955.

The rest of the long Cub production years, which ended in 1979, was marked by modest production figures of mostly less than an annual average of 3,000. Total production of Farmall Cubs and variations

Australian Farmall Model AM ad

Above: *The AM was an Australian-made version of the North American Model M.*

1941 Farmall MD

Right: *Diesel power was introduced for the 1941 Farmall M with the MD model. The four-cylinder engine shared the same bore and stroke as the gasoline and distillate versions. The MD started on gasoline and was switched over to diesel high compression and diesel fuel injection as the motor warmed. Collector Alan Smith of McHenry, Illinois, bought this tractor locally and restored it.*

Farmall MD
The efficiencies of diesel fuel compared with gas or kerosene was a draw for the more expensive MD. The tractor's fuel-injection pump is seen just rear of the fan shroud. The two vertical levers just in the front of the gear shift were used to change the engine to run on diesel after starting on gasoline.

Farmall M tire shields
Tire shields were a Model M option.

during its thirty-two years of production was 252,997 tractors. Cub Lo-Boy tractors, made with reduced clearance for lawn, industrial, and other special uses, were also made in substantial numbers after 1954.

The Cub holds the honor of the longest production run of any tractor made in the United States.

The Big Standards: W-9 and Kin

At the opposite end of the farm power spectrum from the tiny Cubs were the big standard-tread machines built for the really heavy pulling on large farms. The massive W-9, WD-9, and their nearby relatives are more closely related to IH crawler tractors than they are to row-crop tractors as their engines began in the track-type tractors.

The W-9 was introduced in 1940 as a big 44-hp standard-tread workhorse. It packed the four-cylinder 4.40x5.50-inch (110x137.5-mm) bore-and-stroke 335-ci (5,487-cc) engine common to the IH T-9 crawler. In 1945, the W-9 was joined by the WD-9 diesel version of the same 335-ci (5,487-cc) engine with a compression ratio of 15.6:1. The engine was pure IH diesel, starting on gasoline at low compression and converting quickly to diesel high compression as it warmed. The WD-9 as equipped with full rubber was priced at $1,945 when it came along in 1945. It marked a trend toward more use of diesel engines in large farm tractors where their increased fuel efficiency would soon pay back the higher initial investment.

A W-9 designed for use in rice fields was also introduced in 1945 as the WR-9 and WDR-9 Rice Field Specials. The rice models came on 15.00x34-inch (37.5x85-cm) tires rather than the usual 14.00x34-inch (35x85-cm) tires on the W-9 and WD-9. Extra deep lugs on the big tires helped them pull through the soft rice fields. Optionally available were 18.00x26-inch (45x65-cm) single rear tires or dualled 14.00x32-inch (35x80-cm) rears. The rice tractors came with full-tire-width, flat-topped fenders with front shields to keep mud from accumulating on the operator's platform. They were equipped with hand-operated clutches and foot-operated "decelerators" to slow or stop them quickly when negotiating levees. The Rice Field Specials could be fitted with remote control hydraulics for fingertip control of pulled implements.

The industrial versions of the 9 Series were the I-9 and ID-9 tractors. Their major difference from the W-9 and WD-9 were heavy cast rear wheels outfitted with 13.00x32-inch (32.5x80-cm) tires.

Super versions of the W-9, WD-9, WR-9, and WDR-9 replaced the earlier 9 Series in 1953 and were made until 1956. They were rated at 64 belt hp, achieved through an increase in the bore of the engine for a bore and stroke of 4.50x5.50 inches (112.5x137.5 mm).

A total of 74,141 of the 9 Series tractors, including the W-9, WD-9, WR-9, WDR-9, I-9, ID-9 and their Super versions, were built between 1940 and 1954. Of that total, some 8,435 were the Super versions made in 1953 and 1954.

If it needed a demonstration of the need for more power in farm tractors, IH now had that proof with the success of the big 9 Series tractors. The 1950s witnessed the start of the horsepower race in farm tractors as many farm operators, working with ever-tightening margins, consolidated into larger units run by fewer people needing larger machines.

Farmall H operator's view

Above, top: *The operator had a good view of the H's two-row cultivator.*

Farmall H grille

Above, bottom: *Industrial designer Raymond Loewy styled the H.*

1940 Farmall H

Left: *Roland Henik's father traded in a Farmall Regular on this 1940 Farmall H before World War II. The Mount Vernon, Iowa, farmer has used the tractor on his own farm in the intervening fifty-eight years. The two-plow H shared the same frame size with the more powerful M so they could both mount the same implements. Power was about 20 drawbar hp in Nebraska tests. More than 425,000 Farmall H tractors were made 1939 to 1952.*

McCormick-Deering O-4
Above: *The two-plow McCormick-Deering O-4 was the Farmall H equivalent in the standard-tread orchard series. Complete shielding helped this tractor slip through close-growing trees with minimum damage to the crop, the tractor, or the operator. Related to the O-4 were the McCormick-Deering W-4 standard-tread two-plow tractor and the International I-4 industrial version.*

McCormick-Deering O-4 operator's seat
Facing page, top: *Riding on a seat lowered and extended to the rear, the orchard tractor operator enjoyed a shielded position from which to drive the O-4. The solid front rims kept branches out. Verlan Heberer of Belleville, Illinois, owns this tractor.*

McCormick-Deering O-4 gauges
Facing page, bottom: *Shields protected the gauges on the O-4 from tree limbs.*

Cultivating soybeans

Above: *Soybeans and other row crops could be carefully cultivated with the Farmall C. It had the crop clearance needed to lay-by corn at a late-growth stage. A total of 66,216 Farmall Cs were made between 1948 and 1951 when the Super C was introduced. Another 112,006 Super Cs were made from 1951 to 1954.* (Photo courtesy State Historical Society of Wisconsin #WhiIK-2647-LL)

1948 Farmall C with front-mounted planter

Left: *IH replaced the Farmall B with the Model C in 1948. It was a tricycle machine like the B, but used large tires on straight axles like the H and M. The operator's seat and the steering wheel were centered on a platform above the transmission. New too was a Touch-Control hydraulic system for controlling front- and rear-mounted implements. Two levers just above the steering column helped make implement control convenient. The two-row planter was in plain view of the operator. Still equipped with the four-cylinder 3x4-inch (75x100-mm) engine found in the A and B, the C's rpm was stepped up to 1,650 for about 15 drawbar hp.* (Photo courtesy State Historical Society of Wisconsin #WhiI-2431-LL)

Farmall Cub crop clearance

Above: *Axle gearing similar to the first Farmall raised the rear axle high off the ground. Tread was adjustable between 40 and 56 inches (100–140 cm). It was powered with a 60-ci (983-cc) four-cylinder engine of 2.625x2.75 inches (65.625x68.75 mm) bore and stroke turning at 1,600 rpm. Drawbar pull was about 6 hp. It could pull one 12-inch (30-cm) bottom plow. Fitted with a belly-mount mower, the Cub is still one of the favorite estate-sized tractors in use in the United States.*

1949 Farmall Cub

Right: *The smallest Farmall holds the record for the longest production run of any U.S.-made tractor. It was produced thirty-two years straight with a total of 252,997 Cubs made in its 1947 to 1979 production run. Similar to the Farmall A in design, the Cub was a single-row cultivating tractor with its engine and drive components on the left and the operator's seat on the right. Lawrance N. Shaw, professor of Agricultural Engineering at the University of Florida at Gainesville, Florida, uses his Cub to pull a vegetable transplanter he has developed.*

Chapter 8

The Horsepower Race

Today Farmalls are the most popular tractors in America. Most of the first million are still at work. Designed as a basic, all-purpose power unit for a complete line of implements, the Farmall tractor made possible complete mechanization of every farm job.
—Farmall H, M, and MD brochure, 1940s

Above: **1956 Farmall 300**

1954 Farmall 400
Left: *The Farmall Super M and Super M-TA were replaced in 1954 with the handsome Farmall 400. Don Rimathe of Huxley, Iowa, grew up on this 400, which has been on the farm since purchased new by his father, Roy.*

Consolidation of farms into larger units starting in the late-1940s and 1950s provided a new challenge to IH and other tractor makers. IH sought to provide more powerful and more efficient tractors to help fewer farmers operate larger acreages and reduce their power costs.

The post–World War II period saw a growing specialization in cash grain farming such as growing corn, small grains, and soybeans as cash crops without the usual pattern of livestock enterprises as part of a general farming operation. This movement was focused in the central U.S. corn belt in Illinois, Iowa, Indiana, and overlapping into parts of the surrounding states of Nebraska, Minnesota, Wisconsin, Michigan, Ohio, Kentucky, Tennessee, and Missouri. The area was home turf for IH Farmalls and their corn-cultivating capabilities. It's where the Farmall with its "talented" versatility had at last replaced the horse.

With the horse gone from the farm, the need to keep horse pasture for the draft animals was eliminated and that acreage could now be put into crops. Other economic factors at work included the availability of commercial fertilizers at lower costs so a farm's fertility level could now be maintained—even increased—without livestock manure.

Soybeans were starting to be grown as a cash crop in the center of the corn belt from about 1930 on. Since soybeans needed to be processed into meal prior to feeding to cattle and hogs as a protein source, soybeans were sold off the farm and bought as meal for livestock production.

Soybeans are a legume like clover and alfalfa, and they could replace hay crops in a crop rotation and provide needed nitrogen for the corn crop to follow. Ag colleges confirmed it, and one by one at first, then in droves, many corn belt farmers got out of their small livestock operations in the early 1950s, pulled out the fences, and specialized in what soon became extensive cash grain production. That was especially true in the areas with vast tracts of deep, fertile prairie soil. Without the morning and evening livestock chores, farmers' productive days were longer. They gained more crop land and available time when they no longer had to put up three or more crops of hay for the livestock each growing season.

A growing market for larger, more productive Farmalls was appearing right on IH's home ground. Was it up to the challenge? Opting for an incremental approach, IH proceeded cautiously, starting with its then-current models. The only really new models introduced by IH post–World War II were small-horsepower models designed for small "one-horse" farms.

Supers Up the Power Curve

IH began tweaking its entire line starting in 1951 when it announced its two-plow Farmall Super C. The engine bore was increased by 0.125 inches (3.125 mm) to 3.125 inches (78.125 mm) or to a displacement of 122.7 ci (2,010 cc). The updates added 2 hp to the nimble little machine, bringing it up to 20.72 drawbar hp.

The Super C also introduced double disk brakes to the Farmall line. The new disc brakes used tractor motion to help apply the brake. An upholstered seat with variable spring and a two-way shock absorber were signs of improvements to come on later models. A couple of years later, the Super C got the new IH two-point Fast Hitch as an option, which simplified integral equipment attachment. Farmers liked the "back in, pick up and go," ease of hitching implements with the two-point Fast Hitch as compared with the clumsy three-point hitch of some competitors.

Also available optionally on the Super C was the adjustable wide-front and magneto ignition. Most desired equipment, including Touch-Control lift, starter, and lights, PTO, belt pulley, and disk brakes, came standard on the Super C. Some 112,006 Super C Farmalls were made between 1951 and 1954.

The Super A-1 received a boost in engine displacement to 122.7 ci (2,010 cc) by increasing the bore to 3.125 inches (78.125 mm), thus also boosting drawbar horsepower. Just less than 6,000 Farmall Super A-1s were made in 1954.

IH also announced the Super W-6 and Super WD-6 tractors in 1951. They too got power boosts to 46 drawbar hp.

Farm tractors with 50+ drawbar hp were rare as the 1950s dawned. Most tractors tested at Nebraska

1953 Farmall Super H
The Super H, made only from 1953 to 1954, was an improved version of the Farmall H introduced in 1939. This Super H poses proudly in downtown Chicago, Illinois, in front of the site where Cyrus McCormick built his first reaper factory, on the banks of the Chicago River just off Michigan Avenue.

1953 Farmall Super H

Above: *Max Armstrong, WGN Radio farm broadcaster from Chicago, displays his 1953 Farmall Super H in downtown Chicago, Illinois. Max brought the tractor from his home farm near Owensville, Indiana.*

Farmall Super H horsepower increase

Right: *The Super H got a horsepower boost of about 18 percent above the H when the new model was introduced in 1953. Engineers increased the H's cylinder bore from 3.375 to 3.50 inches (84.375 to 87.50 mm) giving the engine a displacement of 164 ci (2,686 cc) and 24 drawbar hp. Double disk brakes replaced the drum brakes of the old H. A deluxe hydraulic seat, Lift-All hydraulics, PTO, belt pulley, lights, and electric starting were all standard features on the Super H. Fewer than 32,000 of the model were made in 1953 and 1954.*

then were in the 20–30 hp range. IH's big W-9 Series finally passed the 50-hp mark in 1953 when it got more power, and was designated the Super W-9. The Super versions of the W-9, WD-9, WR-9, and WDR-9 were rated at 57 drawbar hp, achieved through an increase in engine bore from 4.50 to 5.50 inches (112.5 to 137.5 mm). The Super 9 Series was made until 1956.

The H-sized tractors were converted to the Farmall Super H and Super W-4 in 1953. They could pull 33.4 drawbar hp. Just fewer than 32,000 Super H tractors were made during its two-year production in 1953 and 1954.

A power kick of about 10 hp moved the M tractors to the 46-hp neighborhood when they were re-badged as Supers in 1952. They were the Farmall Super M, Super M-D diesel, and a new Farmall Super M-LPG. More than 75,500 Super M and its variations were made during 1952 and 1953.

Torque Amplifier and the Super M-TA

Announced in 1953 was the Farmall Super M-TA. The Super M-TA was a Super M equipped with the new lever-operated Torque Amplifier transmission that permitted on-the-go shifting to a lower range in each of its five gears, amounting to ten forward and two reverse speeds. There were nearly 27,000 Farmall Super M-TAs made in 1954.

The TA was a planetary gear arrangement located in the clutch housing and connected to the input shaft of the five-speed transmission. Forward speed was reduced by about 32 percent and pull was increased by about 48 percent when in the "low" TA position. TA was soon available on the Farmall Super MD-TA and the McCormick W6-TA. The Torque Amplifier transmission was an IH exclusive and was offered for many years on IH tractors of less than 80 hp.

IH also introduced its independent PTO in 1954. It was direct driven from the engine and was engaged with a lever working an independent clutch. Live, or independent, PTOs continued to revolve even when the tractor clutch was disengaged so PTO implements could operate independent of ground travel.

Numbered Models Again

Another facelift, confined mainly to the sheet metal and new model badges, introduced the Hundred Series in 1954, with the debut of the Farmall 200, the replacement for the Super C. Nebraska tests gave it 20.92 drawbar hp flowing from the four-cylinder 3.125x4.00-inch (78.125x100-mm) 123-ci (2,015-cc) IH engine turning at 1,650 rpm. It weighed 3,541 lb (1,593 kg) at test. Production totals for the Farmall 200 and International 200 are figured at 13,726 from 1954 to 1956 when they were replaced.

The Farmall 200 was the first Farmall to use numerical model numbers since the numbered F Series was replaced with the Letter Series in 1939 and 1940. The subtle styling change for the Hundred Series included a bolder look achieved by enlarging the size of the horizontal slots in the radiator grill and adding to it two centered vertical slots. Chromed model number and name plates helped dress up the new models. Larger, chrome IH symbols graced the top of the front hood of the new models.

New Series, New Models

In 1955, the Farmall 100 Series replaced the Super A-1, the 300 Series the Super H, the 400 Series the Super M, and the W-400 Series the Super W-6 Series. New to the model lineup was the International 300, a low-profile utility tractor of Super H size that soon became a favorite loader tractor found on many farms that still had livestock. The International 300 utility seated the operator forward of the differential housing, straddling the transmission housing, much like the arrangement on the Ford and Ferguson tractors of the day. More than 33,175 International 300 utility tractors were made 1955 to 1956.

The Torque Amplifier was available on the 300 Series and the IH two-point hitch and hydraulics were offered on the 300 and 400 Series tractors. The International 300 utility was available in gas and LPG fuel capabilities. Power was just over 27 drawbar hp in both fuel versions from the 169-ci (2,768-cc) four-cylinder. The engine ran 250 rpm faster in the utility. It weighed 4,413 lb (1,986 kg). The tricycle Farmall 300 used the same engine at 1,750 rpm. It also was available in gas or LPG versions.

The Super A-1 successor, the Farmall 100, kicked out 17.83 drawbar hp from its 123-ci (2,015-cc) four-cylinder gas engine operating at 1,400 rpm. It weighed about 3,000 lb (1,350 kg) as tested at Nebraska. A new feature available on the little 100 gave it the ability to move very slowly for special applications. Hydra-Creeper gave the vegetable crop–oriented 100 a snail's pace of ¼ to 1 mph (0.4–1.6 km/h) at full throttle. It used a PTO-driven hydraulic pump powering the transmission through added speed reduction to give it the "slows" for careful work in the vegetable patch. More than 18,500 Farmall 100s were made during its production from 1954 to 1956.

The big Farmall became the Farmall 400, replacing the Super M-TA. It was a 45.34-drawbar-hp machine with its 264-ci (4,324-cc) four-cylinder engine. At its Nebraska test, it weighed just over 6,500 lb (2,925 kg). It was the first Torque Amplifier–equipped tractor tested at Nebraska and showed ten speeds from 1.7 to 16.7 mph (2.72–26.72 km/h).

The gasoline, diesel, and LPG versions of the Farmall and the International showed about the same horsepower results as the Farmall 400 gasoline. Nearly 40,000 Farmall 400s were made from 1954 to 1956. Another 3,250 of the W-400s were manufactured.

The International 600 replaced the W-9 in the big standard-tractor models. Diesel and gas engines were available in the five-plow, 6,000-lb (2,700-kg) tractor. Updates including double disc brakes, power steering, and Hydra-Touch hydraulics aided its usefulness on large farms. An LPG version, the International 650 LPG, became available in 1956, and it delivered 58.22 drawbar hp at its Nebraska test. Only 1,500 of the big International 600s were made during its brief production from 1956 to 1957. Its replacement, the 650, was built in 1957 and 1958 in numbers approaching 5,000 units.

More changes came to the IH tractor line in 1956. Among them was the addition of Traction Control to the IH's two-point Fast-Hitch. That feature gave the operator better depth and traction control when using rear-mounted implements. Weight could be transferred from the mounted implement to the front tires. Hydraulically aided power steering was a welcome addition to the IH tractors made after 1956.

More Updates, More New Models

In 1956, the Farmall 130, 230, 350, and 450 replaced the even-numbered models of the previous year and were the start of the two-tone Farmalls. A light cream color was used to contrast the red paint scheme, as a background for the Farmall or International trademark on the side of the hood, and as an added contrast on the radiator grill. The 130 replaced the 100, the 230 the 200, the 350 the 300, and the 450 the 400. Power was nudged up on all of the tractors. The In-

Farmall 300 controls

Above: *The Farmall 300 operator was surrounded by controls. The Torque Amplifier lever is at left, the long curved gearshift lever is under the steering wheel, and the throttle is behind the wheel. Engine gauges and a tachometer-mph calculator are beginning to form an instrument cluster in front of the operator.*

ternational 330 utility, which replaced the 300 utility, came along in 1957.

The Farmall Cub for 1956 received new styling. It was tested again at Nebraska that year where it delivered 9.87 drawbar and 10.39 belt hp at 1,800 rpm. That's about one drawbar hp more than the original Cub of 1947, proof that the model was the right tractor for its market.

The new Farmall 130 of 1956, the fourth generation of the Farmall A, showed 19.91 drawbar hp in its Nebraska test, compared with 17.83 hp for the previous Model 100. It was tested at a weight of 3,015 lb (1,357 kg). The Farmall 130 and International 130s built from 1956 to 1958 totaled about 9,750 tractors.

The Farmall 230 of 1956 tested at 25 drawbar hp compared with 20.92 for the Farmall 200. The 4-hp gain apparently came from a boost in operating rpm of 150 rpm to 1,800 on its 123-ci (2,015-cc) engine. The 230 was the fourth generation of the Farmall C, which began in 1948 with a drawbar power pull of only 15 hp. Some 7,450 International and Farmall 230s were produced from 1956 to 1958.

The Farmall 350, great-grandson of the famous

1956 Farmall 300
Chrome dolled-up the Farmall 300, which replaced the Super H in late 1954. Henry L. Nunnikhoven of Pella, Iowa, bought this Farmall 300 new, farmed with it for ten years, and recently restored it. His 300 has Torque Amplifier, which gave it two speeds in each of its five transmission speeds. Independent or live PTO came standard as did starter and lights. The IH two-point hitch was an option on the machine. The Farmall 300 developed just over 27 drawbar hp, or about 3 hp more than the Super H. New styling with bolder grille slots and vertical stripes marked the grille work of the tractor.

Farmall H of 1939 vintage, finally got a diesel engine in 1956. It was a departure from normal IH practice of only using the firm's own engines. The Farmall 350 diesel was powered with a 193-ci (3,161-cc) four-cylinder made by Continental, developing a couple of horsepower less than the IH gas four-cylinder 175-ci (2,867-cc) engine used in the series. An LPG version of the IH engine was also available. At the close of Farmall 350 production in 1958, just over 16,800 of the row-crop tractors were made. Its International 350 standard sibling totaled another 18,000 tractors.

The Farmall 450 of 1956, with its roots tracing back to the M, was also tested at Nebraska in 1956. It had gained a couple of horsepower compared with the Farmall 400 it replaced, and it was coming close to being a 50-hp tractor. The Nebraska tests of the Farmall 450 diesel showed 45.17 drawbar and 48.75 belt hp. The gas 450 put out 55.28 belt hp and the LPG 450 created 54.12 belt hp. The original Farmall M of 1939 debuted at 34.44 drawbar hp, so the seventeen years of tweaking the tractor added nearly 10 hp to its brawn. More than 25,550 Farmall 450s were made along with about 1,800 International 450 standards between 1956 and 1958.

The International 330 utility gasoline, introduced in 1957, was most closely related in size to the Farmall 350. The utility machine had a smaller 135-ci (2,211-cc) four-cylinder engine with a 3.25x4.0625-inch (81.25x101.5625-mm) bore and stroke turning at 2,000 rpm. Power was 31.77 drawbar and 34.24 belt hp, making it somewhat smaller than the Farmall 350 and somewhat stronger than the Farmall 230. It was only produced for about a year until big changes were made in the IH lineup. The International 330 utility was built in numbers just over 4,260 in 1957 and 1958.

Change From the Inside Out

Beginning in 1958, IH introduced new models with major re-engineering. Chief among the changes were new 460 and 560 Farmall and International models sporting new six-cylinder engines in either gas or diesel versions. It was the first time IH had used six-cylinder engines in its row-crop tractors, and the move offered the potential of higher horsepower ratings for its best-selling tractors.

The hydraulic pump, by now a serious part of tractor systems, was moved inside the transmission case from its previous engine-block location. A crankcase oil cooler was added to help dispel heat from the hard-working engines. Steering was reconfigured from the over-the-top position of the early Farmall; the steering shaft was now placed along the engine siderail. There it connected to a worm drive inside the front bolster where steering was hydraulically aided.

There were, of course, styling changes on the new tractors as well. The Farmall 140, 240, 340, 460, 560, and 660 had a new flat radiator grill featuring bold horizontal bars. The cream-colored accent now swept back from the grill and shroud along the sides of the hood to the instrument console. Model designations were placed on the radiator shroud in chrome numerals mounted on a red oval. Operator comfort was aided with a backrest added to the tractor seats. Neat-

1954 Farmall 400
The Farmall Super M and Super M-TA were replaced in 1954 with the handsome Farmall 400. Under the new sheet metal was the same 264-ci (4,324-cc) IH engine which applied 36 hp to the drawbar. LPG was added to gasoline, distillate, and diesel as a fuel option.

1954 Farmall 400
The Farmall 400 weighed 6,500 pounds (2,925 kg). The Torque Amplifier was retained, giving the 400 a range of ten speeds from 1.7 to 16.7 mph (2.7–26.7 km/h).

Farmall 400 two-point hitch
The 400 featured the new IH two-point hitch with drawbar component.

Farmall 400 operator's controls
The 400 featured a full array of operator's controls.

Farmall 400 wheel weights
Front-wheel weights and front-end weights were needed when using the new rear two-point hitch for attaching heavy integral implements. IPTO (independent power take-off), or live PTO, was a new feature for the tractor. "What I know about farming I learned on that tractor," says Rimathe of his Farmall 400, which he learned to drive at the age of nine.

looking instrument consoles were positioned near the steering columns.

The smallest tractor in the new series, the Farmall 140, was a 21.25-drawbar-hp tractor most resembling the old Farmall A. It bore an IH four-cylinder 122.7-ci (2,010-cc) engine with a bore and stroke of 3.125x4.00 inches (78.125x100 mm) turning at 1,400 rpm. The Farmall and International 140s were built for twenty-one years with production ending in 1979 after more than 63,000 of the one-row tractor had been made.

The Farmall 240 was powered with the same 122.7-ci (2,010-cc) engine as in the 140, but it turned over at 2,000 rpm to produce its 28.07 drawbar hp test pull. Some 3,700 Farmall 240 row-crop tractors were made from 1958 to 1961. The 240 also came in an International utility version whose production reached more than 10,320 units through 1962.

The Farmall 340 used a 135-ci (2,211-cc) four-cylinder 3.25x4.0625-inch (81.25x101.5625-mm) gasoline engine to produce 31.76 drawbar hp in its Nebraska test. A Farmall 340 diesel of similar power was also offered. The Farmall 340 accounted for nearly

7,500 tractors made by IH between 1958 and 1963. The International 340s were more popular, with more than 12,000 made in that period.

Six-Cylinder 460 and 560

The Farmall 460 was powered with a six-cylinder 3.5625x3.6875-inch (89.0625x92.1875-mm) IH gas engine of 221 ci (3,620 cc) running at 1,800 rpm. It produced 45.38 drawbar hp during Nebraska tests. Diesel and LPG versions were available producing similar power results on test. International 460 utility versions were available in gas-, LPG-, and diesel-powered tractors. Tractor production records kept in the IH archives show more than 32,500 Farmall 460s made between 1958 and 1963. Another 11,591 units of the International 460 standards were made.

The big IH row-crop tractor of 1958 was the Farmall 560. Its popular diesel model used the six-cylinder 3.6875x4.39-inch (92.1875x109.75-mm) bore-and-stroke 281-ci (4,603-cc) IH diesel. It produced 54.86 drawbar and 59.48 belt hp on Nebraska test. The gasoline Farmall 560 with the 263-ci (4,308-cc) engine tested at 63.03 belt hp; the LPG version

Two-tone Farmalls
A second color was added to the IH paint scheme in 1956 with the introduction of the 130, 230, 350, and 450 Farmall models. Light cream color highlighted the grilles and side panels on the series. This wide-front Farmall is participating in the 1963 National Plowing Match near Vandalia, Illinois.

measured a few horsepower less.

The 560 tractors soon developed serious transmission problems and were the subject of a massive and expensive IH warranty recall-rebuild program. Transmissions in the 560 Series had been changed little from previous lower-horsepower models, and the big 263-ci (4,308-cc) six overpowered it, resulting in failures. Although IH fixed them all, the fiasco hurt the tractor maker's reputation at a time it could ill afford a black eye.

Once fixed, however, the 560 tractors soldiered on to become a popular and well-regarded tractor. IH made and sold more than 65,500 Farmall 560s from 1958 to 1963. Another 5,600 of the standard-tread version were sold during the same time period.

Top dog of the new tractor model introductions was the big International 660 standard, replacing the 650. The 660 diesel's six-cylinder 281-ci (4,603-cc)

engine and sturdy drivetrain applied 71.38 drawbar and 78.78 belt hp. It weighed nearly 5 tons (4,500 kg) as tested. IH used planetary drives on the outer axles, a feature not seen before on IH tractors. The 660 gasoline and LPG versions were capable of nearly two horsepower more than the diesel tractor. IH sold 7,000 of the big standard International 660 between 1959 and 1963.

The pace of IH tractor development quickened as the 1960s came and went. In 1958 IH sacrificed its lead as the number one farm equipment maker to John Deere. Now it had to play a game of catch up with a suddenly aggressive Deere & Company if it was to regain its lead.

Chapter 9

Bold Moves Toward the Future

When you buy your new tractor, remember that you are choosing a new partner for your farming business. *Be sure you pick a thrifty partner, one that will help you* make money *and* save money.
—Farmall ad, 1941

Above: **1976 International 4366 Turbo Diesel**

1959 Farmall 560 Diesel
Left: *A new flat radiator grille with "ladder" bars marked the new IH tractors introduced in 1958. The big row-crop 460 and 560 Farmalls got six-cylinder engines. This 560 had the 281-ci (4,602-cc) IH diesel giving it nearly 55 drawbar hp. Jon Kinzenbaw, IH collector and farm implement maker of Williamsburg, Iowa, rebuilt this 560 to like-new condition.*

International Harvester finally took some giant steps toward its future in 1959 when it opened a new Farm Equipment Research and Engineering Center located south of Hinsdale, Illinois. The 442-acre (177-hectare) site was to emphasize research design and development engineering, and was said to be the largest facility of its kind in the world.

Engineering questions for new tractors, their systems, and accessories were waiting for answers. Hinsdale engineers would address them as new engines, hydraulics, transmissions, and powertrains were proposed and developed for increasingly powerful tractors. Four-wheel drive, enclosed cabs, turbocharging, and even intercooling of boosted engines were to pose new engineering challenges down the road. Some of that work at Hinsdale paid off in key machines made in IH's last twenty-four years.

New 404 and 504 Farmalls

An IH-engineered three-point hitch with hydraulic draft control was a new feature on the new-from-the-ground-up Farmall 404 and 504 introduced in 1960. IH was joining the swing toward the three-point hitch pioneered by Harry Ferguson on the Ford-Ferguson 9N tractor in 1939. The three-point free-link attachment system became the standard in the industry in 1959 and enhanced the compatibility between equipment and tractors of different manufacture.

IH expanded the use of tractor oil coolers to cool both transmission and hydraulics as increased heat grew with the new larger power demands on both systems. The 504 had an advanced hydrostatic power-steering system that removed the mechanical connection between the steering wheel and the front wheels. New on both tractors were new, more effective, dry-type air cleaners providing easier servicing.

Gas Turbine HT-340

The revolutionary International HT-340 concept tractor was shown at the University of Nebraska's Power and Safety Day at Lincoln, Nebraska, on July 20, 1961. The HT-340 was a gas turbine-powered machine that substituted the conventional internal-combustion engine with an engine more at home in the air than in a tractor. A 60-lb (27-kg) turbine engine made by Solar Aircraft Company, an IH subsidiary at the time, was rated at 80 hp at 57,000 rpm. Reduction gearing dropped the rpm from the "screaming" machine low

enough to drive a hydraulic pump. Hydraulic pressure from the pump powered the ultra-modern tractor through a new, experimental hydrostatic transmission. The hydrostatic drive provided continuously variable speeds for the tractor.

Streamlined fiberglass body panels made the HT-340 a sleek, low-profile beauty. Turbine exhaust gases exited at the top front of the tractor. The machine remained an experimental concept tractor, and IH donated its "jet" tractor to the Smithsonian Institution in Washington, D.C., on September 1, 1967.

Four-Wheel Drive and Turbocharger Too!

IH farm tractors took an enormous leap in power and size in 1961. IH brought its huge 4300 construction model four-wheel-drive tractor over to its farm side. The IH 4300 gave notice to competitors that larger, more-powerful farm tractors were cards it too could play. Chief competitor John Deere's 8010 four-wheel drive appeared in 1959 and stayed around until 1964 as the 8020.

The International 4300 weighed in at nearly 30,000 lb (13,500 kg). It packed a 300-hp IH six-cylinder turbocharged 817-ci (13,382-cc) diesel, and featured a torque converter coupled to a six-range power shift transmission. It was the first IH farm tractor to offer four-wheel drive and a turbocharged engine. Nebraska tests showed 214.23 drawbar hp at 2,100 rpm. IH engineers developed a ten-bottom mounted plow for the new tractor's three-point hitch. Steering was through all wheels for crab steer, or through just the front wheels for conventional steering.

A turbocharger's magic is its ability to supply an engine with more oxygen so it can burn more fuel and make more power on each turn of the crankshaft. Turbine blades spun by exhaust gases compress air for combustion and ram it into the engine at pressures above normal atmospheric pressures. Provided with additional fuel, a turbocharged engine can produce more power than one of equal displacement that is not turbocharged. Turbochargers were used extensively on World War II aircraft to boost their power and altitude ceilings.

International 4100 Series

The designed-for-the-farm International 4100 four-wheel drive was ready to replace the massive International 4300 in 1965. It was powered with a more mod-

Farmall evolution

More than thirty-four years of Farmall evolution shows in the features on the 1959 five-plow Farmall 560 diesel. For the first time a Farmall tractor used a six-cylinder engine. Power steering had become standard, and the operator had a seat designed for comfort. And, the tractor pulled three more plows than the original Farmall of 1924.

est 429-ci (7,027-cc) six-cylinder turbocharged diesel engine. Nebraska tests showed 110.82 drawbar and 116.15 PTO hp produced by the tractor at 2,400 rpm. It came with a factory-installed cab with built-in heating and air conditioning.

The yellow-and-white 4100 was replaced in 1972 with the red-and-white 4166. The power of the In-

ternational 4166 was up to 130.7 drawbar and 150.63 PTO hp thanks to a larger, 436-ci (7,142-cc) six-cylinder turbocharged diesel.

Farmall 706 and 806

The new Farmall 706 and 806 tractors announced in 1963 boasted new powertrains designed to handle heavier pulling loads and new hydraulic systems with three separate circuits to handle power brakes, power steering, and mounted equipment. The operator's platform was cleared by moving shift levers to the side of the steering wheel support column. The operator's position was moved ahead of the rear axle to provide a better ride.

The 706 and 806 also offered a factory-fitted part-time front-wheel-drive attachment. The Farmall 706 delivered 67.55 drawbar and 72.42 PTO hp from its 282-ci (4,619-cc) six-cylinder diesel engine at 2,300 rpm. The big six-plow 806 was a strong 85-drawbar-hp machine powered by a six-cylinder 361-ci (5,913-cc) diesel. Its optional front-wheel drive added some 30 percent to its traction. Both models were available until 1967 in Farmall and International versions. IH bragged that the Farmall 806 was "The World's Most Powerful Row-Crop Tractor."

Horsepower Milestone

IH upped the ante to the 100-hp level in a two-wheel-drive tractor with the Farmall 1206 of 1965. The 1206 set another record for IH as well: It was the first IH Farmall factory equipped with a turbocharger.

Tested by Nebraska at 10,115 lb (4,552 kg), the 1206 showed 99.16 drawbar and 112.64 PTO hp produced by the 361-ci (5,913-cc) turbocharged six-cylinder engine revolving at 2,400 rpm. Along with its other firsts, the 1206 could be factory equipped with a cab, a feature about to bloom on the bigger tractors of the day. The 1206 was made from 1965 to 1967 and was replaced by the re-styled 1256.

Stablemate to the 1206 in 1965 was the smaller Farmall 656. It tested out at 54.35 drawbar and 61.52 PTO hp. The four-plow 656 was powered by the IH six-cylinder 281.3-ci (4,608-cc) engine. It was to play a new role a couple of years later.

Hydrostatic Transmission

Using development and engineering work from its 1961 turbine-powered HT-340 experimental tractor, IH announced in 1967 that its Hydrostatic transmission would be available in its 656 tractor. Coupling a piston-type hydraulic pump driven by the engine flywheel to a piston-type hydraulic motor connected directly to a high-low transmission gave the operator infinite speed control in two ranges. Speed control was achieved by setting the S/R, or speed-ratio, lever,

Farmall 560
The 560 offered a clear view ahead for operators.

Farmall 560
Drawbar element in the two-point hitch.

Farmall 560
The Hydra-Touch levers controlled the 560's hydraulics.

located at the left of the steering column. The hydrostatic transmission gave speeds from 0 to 8 mph (0–12.8 km/h) in the low range and up to 21 mph (33.6 km/h) in the high range. In lieu of a clutch, a foot pedal could release the oil pressure and stop the tractor at any time.

Both gasoline and diesel versions of the 656 Hydro were available. Its 263-ci (4,308-cc) six-cylinder gas engine produced 50.78 drawbar and 65.80 PTO hp at 2,300 rpm in Nebraska tests. The diesel 281.3-ci (4,608-cc) six-cylinder produced 66.06 PTO hp at its test. The 656 Hydrostatic model was built from 1967 to 1973.

The Hydrostatic drive was used in several IH models including the Farmall 544 in 1968, and the 1026 and the 826 diesels in 1969. On some of the Hydro tractors, drawbar horsepower tested as much as 20 hp lower than the PTO measurements. A 10-hp differential was more common on gear-drive tractors.

The V-8 1468 Diesel

Included in the eleven tractor models IH introduced in 1971 was the V-8–powered International 1468 diesel, the first IH farm tractor with more than six cylinders. It was a distinctive-looking machine with its two chrome stacks exiting the exhaust manifolds on both sides of the wide motor. The 550-ci (9,009-cc) eight-cylinder diesel gave it 126.91 drawbar and 145.77 PTO hp when tested at Nebraska in 1971. It became the International 1568 in 1974 and delivered 133.79 drawbar and 150.70 PTO hp on test.

Farmall Name is Dropped

IH discontinued the use of the historic "Farmall" name on its tractors in 1973, some fifty years after the first Farmalls were produced in 1923 for the 1924 marketing year. Use of the valuable trade name had declined as tractors got larger and eschewed the tricycle front for wide-front stability. The Farmall name was reserved for the tricycle tractors.

The Internationals with their wide front ends could still handle row-crop work if their front axles were adjustable to the crop row width. With the advent of the three-point hitch and hydraulic lift and depth control, most row-crop cultivators were being mounted at the rear of the tractor. Back there, out of sight of a forward-looking operator, the rear-mounted cultivator could do a good job of cultivating—if the operator had achieved the faith that practice brought, that the cultivator was where the operator thought it was, still behind the tractor and following the row.

Articulated Steiger Four-Wheel Drive

IH desired to sell more big, four-wheel-drive tractors than it could make, so it turned to the Steiger Company of Fargo, North Dakota. IH bought into Steiger in 1972, and in 1973, Steiger made the International 4366. It featured a turbocharged 225-hp IH six-cylinder 455-ci (7,453-cc) diesel engine. It was of articulated-steer design with the operator enclosed in a cab at the rear of the front unit.

The International 4568 of 1975 was of similar design but featured the big IH 798-ci (13,071-cc) V-8 turbocharged diesel of 228.01 drawbar and 235.72 PTO hp. The two tractors stayed in the line as the International 4386 and the 4586 in 1977. A bigger version of the V-8, a 800-ci (13,104-cc) diesel, was used in the 4786 of 1979, making it a 350-hp tractor.

The Steiger-built units disappeared from the line in 1982 when IH sold its 30 percent interest in Steiger to help dispose of growing company indebtedness.

The Last Hurrah

One of the last original ideas the waning International

Futurisitic tractor

Right, top: *IH engineering research produced this revolutionary HT-340 gas turbine–powered tractor in 1961. A 60-pound (27-kg) Solar Aircraft Company turbine engine "screamed" at 57,000 rpm to produce 80 hp through reduction gearing in the tractor. A new hydrostatic transmission gave it variable speeds. The concept tractor was not produced although the hydrostatic transmission showed up in later IH tractors. In 1967, IH gave the HT-340 to the Smithsonian Institution in Washington, D.C.* (Photo courtesy State Historical Society of Wisconsin #WhiI-1482-HH)

1965 International 4100

Right, bottom: *Four-wheel drive, turbocharging, and a cab with air conditioning all came with the International 4100 introduced in 1965 to replace the earlier and larger International 4300 of 1961. The new 4100 produced 110.82 drawbar and 116.15 PTO hp from its 429-ci (7,027-cc) six-cylinder turbocharged diesel in its Nebraska tests. The 4100 weighed 15,175 pounds (6,829 kg), a relative lightweight compared with the 4300 at 29,815 pounds (13,417 kg). The 4300 had the first turbocharger used on an IH farm tractor. Power from the 4300's 817-ci (13,382-cc) diesel six was measured at 214.23 drawbar hp at Nebraska. Of interest is that the 4100 produced one hp per 130 pounds (58.5 kg) of weight, compared with a ratio of one hp per 500 pounds (225 kg) for the earliest IH tractors.* (Photo courtesy State Historical Society of Wisconsin #WhiI-64-7C-14)

developed was the new 2+2 four-wheel-drive tractor introduced in 1979. Its concept was bold, combining the strengths of a four-wheel-drive tractor and the maneuverability of a row-crop tractor into one all-purpose machine—the concept had shades of the Farmall of 1924. The International 3388 and 3588 models of the 2+2 Series arrived in 1979. Using a front and rear section hinged near the center, or articulated, the machine could turn in a 31.5-foot (9.45-meter) circle—agile for a four-wheel-drive machine.

The 2+2 used some existing IH components in its construction. The rear section containing the Control Center, or operator's cab, was the rear axle and drivetrain section of the 88 Series production tractors. The front half with the engine was designed with the engine projecting far forward of the front axle to shift weight to the front wheels for better weight distribution under load.

The point of articulation, or hinging, between the units was just in front of the windshield. The operator sat behind the front unit so he or she could see where the tractor was going. The engine was in a sealed compartment in front to reduce the noise it transmitted to the operator's cab. The cab had insulation and sound deadening to make the Control Center a peaceful place to handle the horsepower for long hours.

The 3388 was powered by a 130-hp six-cylinder 436-ci (7,142-cc) turbocharged engine. The 3588 used a 466-ci (7,633-cc) version of the engine with a longer stroke to turn out 150 hp. In 1980, a 180-hp 3788 was announced. It was upgraded to the 6788 in 1983.

In 1982, two 2+2 models were updated. The 6388 replaced the 3388 and the 6588 replaced the 3588. Power ratings remained the same, but ease of shifting was improved with an electro-hydraulic brake.

Super 70 models of the 2+2 tractors were announced at the fall 1984 farm shows. The 7288 was rated at 210 hp, the 7488 at 235 hp. They were never produced, however. IH was dangling at the end of its financial rope and was about to be purchased by Tenneco Inc. and added to its J. I. Case Company subsidiary.

Humpty Had a Great Fall. . . .

The decline had started years earlier. IH had not performed as well financially as its competitors for many years, according to Barbara Marsh, author of *A Corporate Tragedy: The Agony of International Harvester Company*. In 1979, its last decent year, IH ranked twenty-seventh on the Fortune 500 with sales of $8.4 billion and profits of $369 million. Nearly 98,000 people worked for IH around the globe, including 64,000 in the United States. The firm ran forty-one plants worldwide. It was the leading North American producer of medium- and heavy-duty trucks, the world's second-largest maker of farm equipment, a major presence in construction equipment, and a top manufacturer of gas turbines.

As Marsh summarizes the problems, a shrinking IH had sales of $3.6 billion in 1983, and was down to 104th on the Fortune 500. Losses came to $485 million that year, amounting to a nearly $3 billion loss from 1980 to 1983. IH was down to 32,000 workers worldwide with 19,000 of them in the United States.

IH's financial migraine did not stop for the cel-ebration of its 150th year in 1981, the anniversary of Cyrus McCormick's famous reaper. To help stem the hemorrhaging of red ink, IH sold off the Cub Cadet garden tractor business to Modern Tool & Die of Cleveland, Ohio, and the Solar Turbine division to Caterpillar. In 1982, IH sold it's 50 percent share in Kimco to Komatsu and the construction equipment business to Dresser Industries. IH's net loss for fiscal 1982 was $1.638 billion. More plant closings and sales followed. By the close of the 1983 fiscal year, two years after it expected to return the profitability, its annual loss was $485 million.

Tenneco Buys IH

In November 1984, Tenneco Inc. announced that it was buying the IH agricultural equipment division to combine with its J. I. Case Company subsidiary. The proud old farm equipment company was biting the dust after more than 150 years of surviving through thick and thin years.

Tenneco paid $260 million in cash and $170 million in preferred stock for IH. Excluded from the sale was the Rock Island, Illinois, Farmall Works, a factory with a capacity of 37,000 tractors per year. It closed on May 15, 1985, after being open since October 1926 when it began to make the famous Farmall tractors.

Case dropped the IH 50 Series and the 2+2 tractors when it put together the new Case-International line. The new owner kept the IH tractors of less than 80 hp and eliminated the IH tractors above 80 hp. Case combined its dealerships with the IH dealerships, eliminated some 400 dealers, and ended up with about 2,300 dealers.

International Harvester Company will be long remembered for the major contributions it made to the farms of the world, helping the farmer produce more food and fiber with less labor and cost. The McCormick reaper gave the company its start in that direction. The revolutionary Farmall tractor, and the long stream of products it spawned, kept IH in the forefront of the industrialization of agriculture approaching the twenty-first century.

May the International Harvester spirit long continue at Case-International.

1995 7220 Case-IH and 1954 Farmall 400—forty years of progress

Don Rimathe of Huxley, Iowa, can contrast the productivity of the tractor his father Ray bought more than forty years ago with the tractor he now operates on the same farm. With the Farmall 400's 45 drawbar horsepower pulling a three-bottom 16-inch plow, his dad could plow nearly seventeen acres per ten-hour day. The 138.9 drawbar horsepower of the Case-IH Magnum gives it power to plow eighty acres in a ten-hour period when hooked to a six-bottom 18-inch plow. That's more than four times as fast as his father could plow in the same amount of time. Rimathe uses a chisel plow instead of a moldboard plow.

Bibliography

Some of the books, periodicals, articles, and papers referred to in researching this book include:

Broehl, Wayne G., Jr. *John Deere's Company: A History of Deere & Company and its Times.* New York: Doubleday, 1984.

Gay, Larry. *Farm Tractors: 1975-1995.* St. Joseph, MI: American Society of Agricultural Engineers, 1995.

Gray, R. B. *The Agricultural Tractor: 1855-1950.* St. Joseph, MI: American Society of Agricultural Engineers, 1975.

Gray, W. C. "Farmall Tractor History." Notes and documents relating to Farmall development and role of Bert R. Benjamin. Chicago: Advertising Department, International Harvester Company, circa 1938. Unpublished manuscript and collection from IH Archives, State Historical Society of Wisconsin.

Hafstad, Margaret R., ed. *Guide to the McCormick Collection.* Madison, WI: The State Historical Society of Wisconsin, 1973.

Hutchinson, William T. *Cyrus Hall McCormick: Vol. 1, Seed-Time, 1809-1856.* N.p.: The Century Co., 1930.

Hutchinson, William T. *Cyrus Hall McCormick. Vol. 2, Harvest, 1856-1884.* N.p.: The Century Co., 1930.

Johnson, Paul C. *Farm Inventions in the Making of America.* Des Moines, IA: Wallace Homestead, 1978.

Johnson, Paul C. *Farm Power in the Making of America.* Des Moines, IA: Wallace-Homestead, 1976.

Klancher, Lee. *International Harvester Photographic History.* Osceola, WI: Motorbooks International, 1996.

Larsen, Lester. *Farm Tractors: 1950-1975.* St. Joseph, MI: American Society of Agricultural Engineers, 1981.

Leffingwell, Randy. *The American Farm Tractor.* Osceola, WI: Motorbooks International, 1991.

Marsh, Barbara. *A Corporate Tragedy: The Agony of International Harvester Company.* New York: Doubleday, 1985.

McCormick, Cyrus. *The Century of the Reaper.* Boston: Houghton Mifflin Co., 1931.

Morrell, T. H. "The Development of Agricultural Equipment PTO Mechanisms." St. Joseph, MI: American Society of Agricultural Engineers paper, 1980.

Muhm, Don. "At 92, 'Father of the Farmall' Tackles New Field," *Des Moines* [IA] *Sunday Register,* Oct. 27, 1963.

Prairie Farmer eds. "Farm Power From Muscle to Motor, Revolution in Rubber, Plows that Made the Prairies, The Better the Fuel . . ." *Prairie Farmer* magazine centennial issue, Jan. 11, 1941.

Wendel, C. H. *Encyclopedia of American Farm Tractors.* Osceola, WI: Motorbooks International, 1992.

Wendel, C. H. *International Harvester—150 Years.* Osceola, WI: Motorbooks International, 1993.

Wormley, Jack. "Bert Benjamin known as 'Father of Farmall.'" *The Jasper County* [Newton, IA] *Farmer,* Feb. 9, 1994.

About the Author

Photographer-author Ralph W. Sanders has photographed tractors for nearly thirty-seven years. He was raised on a central Illinois farm where he had ample opportunity to regularly "exercise" a 1933 Farmall F-12 and a 1948 Farmall C. Helping neighbors bale straw, apply anhydrous ammonia, and shell corn also provided working acquaintances with a Farmall H, Farmall MD, and McCormick-Deering W-9.

Ralph attended the University of Illinois in Urbana and earned his bachelors degree in journalism in 1958. His journalism career began at WCRA radio in Effingham, Illinois; he moved to WDZ radio and then to *The Herald & Review* in Decatur, Illinois. He was Illinois field editor for *Prairie Farmer* magazine from 1964 to 1968, when he joined *Successful Farming* magazine in Des Moines, Iowa, as an associate editor.

In 1974, Ralph followed his passion for photography and became a full-time freelance photographer. His agricultural photographic work has included assignments for *Successful Farming*, Deere & Co., Massey-Ferguson, Kinze Manufacturing, Vermeer Manufacturing, DuPont Agricultural, Monsanto Agricultural, and many others.

Ralph and his wife of thirty-nine years, Joanne, who is the oldest daughter of Lester and Florence Helms of Belleville, Illinois, have seven grown children and seven grandchildren. They have lived in West Des Moines, Iowa, for thirty years. In 1996, they sold their business, Sanders Photographics, Inc., to two of their sons, Scott and Richard. With their extra time, Ralph and Joanne plan to travel more widely and photograph more classic tractors.

Ralph and Joanne already cover up to 10,000 miles each year in the United States and Canada taking photographs for use in calendars and books. This is Ralph's second book with Voyageur Press. His first, *Vintage Farm Tractors*, was published in 1996.